VATCH'S
SOUTH
EAST
ASIAN
COOKBOOK

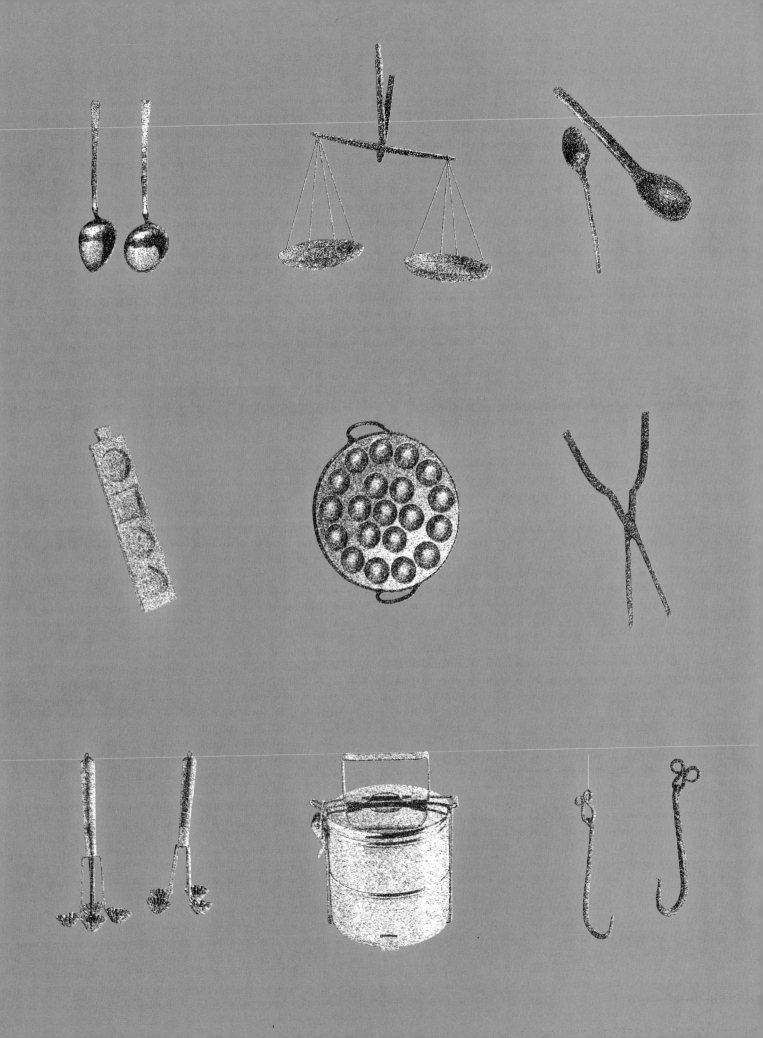

VATCHARIN BHUMICHITR

VATCH'S
SOUTH
EAST
ASIAN
COOKBOOK

WITH PHOTOGRAPHS BY CHRISTINE HANSCOMB
MICHAEL FREEMAN AND VATCHARIN BHUMICHITR

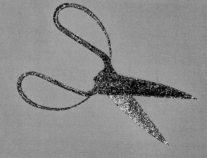

ST. MARTIN'S PRESS
NEW YORK

For all my friends throughout Southeast Asia who helped with this book and for my traveling companions who first shared these recipes

First published in Great Britain in 1997 by Kyle Cathie Limited
20 Vauxhall Bridge Road, London SW1V 2SA

VATCH'S SOUTHEAST ASIAN COOKBOOK
Copyright © Vatcharin Bhumichitr 1997

Food photographs copyright © Christine Hanscomb 1997
Travel photographs on pages 9, 10, 11, 12, 15, 16, 18, 19, 20, 22, 23, 24, 25, 27, 28, 29,30,
50, 52, 53, 54, 56, 57, 59, 60, 83, 84, 85, 86, 108, 109, 110, 113, 114, 134, 137, 138, 140,
142, 143, 160, 162, 163, 169 copyright © Michael Freeman 1997
Travel photographs on pages 7, 8, 14, 17, 26, 31, 55, 61, 80, 82, 87, 106, 111, 112, 115,
132, 135, 136, 139, 141, 164, 167 copyright © Vatcharin Bhumichitr 1997

Library of Congress Cataloging-in-Publication Data
Vatcharin Bhumichitr.
   Vatch's Southeast Asian cookbook / by Vatcharin Bhumichitr. – 1st U.S. ed.
     p.   cm.
   Includes index.
   ISBN 0-312-18274-0
   1. Cookery. Southeast Asian. 2. Food habits–Asia, Southeastern.
3. Asia. Southeastern–Social life and customs.   I. Title.
TX724.5.S68V38   1998
641.5959–dc21   97-33264
                                                                          CIP

First U.S. Edition

10 9 8 7 6 5 4 3 2 1

Styling by Antonia Gaunt
BOOK DESIGN BY THE BRIDGEWATER BOOK COMPANY
Printed in Singapore by Tien Wah Press

CONTENTS

INTRODUCTION

A spicy salad of squid, prawns, mussels and clams after a cooling swim in the Bay of Phangna; a curry steamed in banana leaves in a restaurant overlooking the Mekong at Luang Prabang; Cambodian lemon grass chicken in Siam Reap near the ancient temples of Angkor Wat – the food of Southeast Asia is waiting to be discovered. There are unexpected pleasures, like the sharp Cambodian dip tik marij, a simple mix of salt, pepper and lime juice, the tangy attack of which takes you completely by surprise; or food you may have already tried, like Vietnamese fresh spring rolls that turn out to be even fresher and very much tastier when made in the real Vietnamese way. From rich and creamy Burmese noodles to pungent nonya seafood in Penang and Singapore, there is a new world of flavours and textures that has been hidden away for far too long.

Kitchen knives on sale in Hanoi, Vietnam

I began to think about this book towards the end of the eighties, when it became clear that the tourist flood that had engulfed Thailand would inevitably spread outwards into the surrounding countries. The collapse of worldwide Communism meant that the previously sealed off lands along our borders would soon be open to visitors for the first time in nearly 20 years. When I was young it was enough of an adventure to travel round Thailand; now the whole region was waiting. For some, the term 'Southeast Asia' means all the lands south of China, stretching as far as Japan; for others it stops short at Indonesia or Singapore. Some include Burma in their definitions, others not. There are those who use language or religion as a guide, I have chosen food and have taken my native land as a starting point and included those of our neighbours with whom we have some culinary affinity – Laos, Cambodia, Vietnam, Burma, Malaysia and Singapore.

Of course, there are many different ways in which we are united: all but Vietnam have a common border with Thailand; five share the Mekong River on its journey from China to the sea; three have northern mountain ranges that make up the Golden Triangle, notorious home to hill-tribes, war lords and opium; four

practise an identical form of Buddhism and have near-identical art and architecture, dance and theatre. The one thing that all share is a culinary history that comes from similar agricultural practices and the cultivation of identical crops. With food in mind we are more alike than different.

Historically, wars, invasions, migrations and missionaries also played a part. Kingdoms and empires rose and fell, uniting and dividing and helping the spread of ideas, whether the lofty teachings of the Buddha or the humble knowledge of how to cultivate the mango or cook with coconut milk. The name the French have always preferred for the region, Indo-China, is apt because ours is in many ways the area where those two great cultures meet and merge. It is also not a bad description of Southeast Asian food to say that it is a unique blend of Chinese and Indian elements – with those countries to the West, like Burma, being more Indian, while Vietnam in the East is visibly more Chinese.

Perhaps just as crucial as this East/West split is the division between those who live in the flat river valleys of the South and those who occupy the mountainous areas to the North. Northern food is robust and often hunted and gathered – game and wild herbs, eaten with glutinous or sticky rice – food prepared in ways largely unchanged over the ages, because the peoples of this region are farthest from the sea and the new influences it brings. The South is more populous, with civilizations growing and spreading among the city states, the cultural monuments of which are the region's triumph: Angkor Wat and Pagan, above all. And from the sea came changes – traders bringing spices from other lands, immigrants importing fresh culinary traditions – a steady flow of new things that has made southern cooking a perpetually evolving feast.

What my seven countries do not share is the more recent past when we were separated by the British and French Empires, a division that left Siam, as it then was, the only independent state, a buffer between the two colonial powers. This situation was

**Entrance to the Bayon,
Angkor Wat, Cambodia**

hardly improved by independence, when the Cold War placed some lands in the Western capitalist camp, with others in the grip of either Russia or China. It was a story that slid into nightmare – the Vietnam War, the bombing of Laos, Pol Pot and the Killing Fields. Even Malaysia had a long jungle war to suppress communist guerrillas, while tension between its Malay and Chinese communities led to the break with Singapore. Burma has had 30 years of army rule and Thailand lived through a succession of military coups before achieving some semblance of democratic order.

While all this was going on, one thing was transforming Thailand out of all recognition – tourism. Today, if you haven't visited Thailand, then you will certainly know someone who has, and probably more than once. With so many in love with Thailand's tropical beaches and famously friendly people, and addicted to a cuisine that has now spread throughout the world on a phenomenal scale, it was inevitable that this affection for one Southeast Asian country and its food would generate a desire to visit those countries nearby. Who has not dreamed of seeing the ghostly sculpted heads rising out of the morning mist at Angkor Wat, or longed to watch the flying fishes on the Road to Mandalay? Who has not wondered what life must be like in Hanoi after years of war, or shuddered at the idea of Cambodia with the Khmer Rouge still hidden in the jungle along the Thai border?

About five years ago, the travel pages of Western newspapers began to suggest that dreams of visiting these places might at last be fulfilled, that the lost nations of Southeast Asia were now ready to welcome the outside world. Intrepid travel journalists risked their lives in cities without discotheques to bring back harrowing accounts of slow trains and restaurants without English menus.

Nevertheless, they confirmed the assumption that there was going to be a tourist boom – and soon.

In fact it has happened, though not quite as the pundits predicted. While there are companies that offer quick package tours of the major cultural sites of Cambodia and Vietnam, individual travellers can still face many difficulties. Just getting visas for Burma or Vietnam in most Western capitals can pose serious problems, let alone finding and booking a hotel. For the seasoned visitor to Thailand, however, there is an easy solution to hand – get to Bangkok and book there. Today, Thai Airways International covers the whole region, and there are tour companies in Bangkok which will arrange as much or as little of your time as you choose – and will get you your visa, too, all in 24 hours!

This is precisely the way I did it. I had already been to Malaysia, which was never closed off, but starting in 1994 I decided to make a concerted effort to see all those places that are part of my culture but which had been denied to me for so long. I began with Laos, on our northern border, and the following year visited North Vietnam and Burma. Then I went to Cambodia, which was extraordinary, as, for entirely different reasons, was my last destination, Singapore. It was in many ways a journey from the past to the present and beyond. It was also not unlike the journey of discovery that I had made around Thailand over the past 20 years, as domestic air routes opened up its distant cities, a journey that I have written about in my earlier books on Thai cuisine.

In the same way, this book is a Cook's Tour of Southeast Asia, a food-lover's exploration of seven countries, a highly personal glimpse of the culture and the cuisine of some of the world's most intriguing places. I hope these reports from the front will help those planning to follow, or will at least set in context the meals that you can make from the recipes I have collected on my travels.

Whenever I arrive in a new place I always head straight for its main cultural monument, be it a temple, museum, statue, whatever, then it's off to the biggest market I can find, after which it's usually time to eat, preferably somewhere modest and local. Put them together – the highest art and the humblest food – and you learn a great deal about the people whose land you have come to see, and you know them even better when you learn to cook their food yourself.

My aim with the recipes in this book was to choose only those that can be authentically reproduced in the West. You will find that the great majority of them are simplicity itself, and will be even easier if you take a moment to read the notes that follow which offer some practical advice on equipment and ingredients. After that it's time for our journey – a Vietnamese savoury pancake on the banks of the Purple River, chilli crab on Singapore's East Coast, crispy duck with hot Burmese sauce under a tamarind tree in a garden in Mandalay: I hope you are feeling hungry...

BEFORE YOU BEGIN

EQUIPMENT
Any well-equipped Western kitchen will have everything you need to cope with the great majority of the recipes in this book. Special tools, such as a Cambodian grill or a Thai dipping mould, are explained where they are needed, and any possible substitutes suggested. However, if you intend to cook Southeast Asian food frequently, you will find it helpful to have the following:
- A wok and a shovel-ended stirrer (often sold together).
- An electric rice cooker – anyone in Asia with access to electricity has one.
- A Chinese chopping axe or cleaver.
- A mortar and pestle.
- A steamer – either Chinese bamboo stacking steamers or the conventional Western two-compartment steamer.
- A long-handled mesh strainer, which is used either for lifting food out of oil or water or for dipping ingredients such as noodles into boiling liquid.

TECHNIQUES
PREPARATION All the hard work is in the prior preparation. In principle, everything is chopped into bite-sized pieces, then quickly cooked. The 'cut' used varies according to the ingredient – how hard it is, or what is best needed to release its flavours. Thus a carrot may be finely chopped, while ginger could be slivered into fine matchsticks. A soft, and therefore more delicate, element like tomato will be cut into wedges, but a spring onion will probably be cut into quite large pieces in order to maintain its crunchiness.

Hindu temple, Singapore

STIR-FRYING The most common instruction in this book is to stir-fry. This involves putting the ingredients into the oil in the order that will ensure that each is cooked at the final point; in other words the toughest food first, the softest last. Ideally you should need to give each only a single quick stir before the next ingredient goes in. Never overcook. Be quick and courageous: meats need only to be just cooked through and all vegetables should remain al dente.

STEAMING Steaming is easy to understand but difficult to judge. In general, cooking is complete when a skewer can be cleanly removed from whatever is being steamed with no following liquid. This check can also be used for grilled chicken, etc.

DRY-FRYING Some recipes call for dry-frying, particularly of rice or sesame seeds, etc. This means just what it says: you place the ingredients in a completely dry frying pan or wok and cook them, shaking from time to time to prevent burning, until they are crisp and golden and give off a pleasant aroma. To repeat – never overcook!

SERVING QUANTITIES

Each section of this book contains a number of one-dish meals which are either rice- or noodle-based. The amounts given for these recipes will make exactly that, a meal for one person, so multiply the ingredients by the number of people for which you plan to cater.

All other recipes have been planned on the basis that each will form part of a typical Southeast Asian meal, where four people will share four or five different dishes, plus rice. If you are planning to cook for fewer people, you are best advised to make fewer dishes (minimum three), rather than scale down the quantity of the ingredients in any of the dishes given here.

Some suggestions on how to combine these recipes into full, satisfying and balanced meals are given at the end of the book (see page 188).

INGREDIENTS

The recipes in this book have been carefully limited to dishes that can be authentically produced in Western kitchens using only those ingredients reasonably easily available outside Asia. You must have the basic ingredients and primary flavours listed here before you can begin, but most of these are now sold in ordinary local supermarkets. The more unfamiliar items can be bought in specialist shops, Chinese or Indian, or in some cases now, Thai. Most large towns in Britain have at least one such shop, while those cities in America with large Asian communities have full-scale Asian supermarkets selling everything you need.

A word of warning: many Oriental food products vary widely in intensity of flavour. Some fish sauces and yellow bean sauces are far saltier than others, while no two chillies are equally hot. I have given reasonable, average amounts in these recipes, but when it comes to the final choice of just how much of any ingredient you should use, follow your own taste in deciding whether you like something to be more or less highly flavoured.

BASICS OILS — In the past, a considerable variety of cooking media were used across Southeast Asia: liquid pork fat in Thailand and its nearest neighbours, Indian ghee in parts of Burma and Malaysia, where coconut oil was also used. While these survive in some country cooking, the use of vegetable oil is now almost universal and is recommended here. Only a light flavourless variety such as sunflower oil should be used – olive oil never. Many recipes open with this neutral oil being flavoured with fried garlic or shallots.

The exception is sesame oil, made from crushed sesame seeds, which is used more like a dressing to add flavour to some Vietnamese dishes. While it can be added to stir-fried dishes, its low burning point makes it unsuitable as a frying medium on its own. It is most often sprinkled over already prepared food, adding a strong nutty flavour. The best is made from toasted sesame seeds and is dark-coloured and thick, with a strong aroma of roasted nuts.

Some Burmese food, especially in the region around Pagan, has the distinct taste of locally produced peanut oil. One way to reproduce this would be to add a little of the distinctively flavoured nut oils, such as walnut, used for salads in the West – not the neutral nut cooking oils like highly refined groundnut oil!

RICE — Of the eleven main varieties of rice, only two are commonly used in Southeast Asian cooking. Plain long-grain rice is the most usual, of which the best is Thai fragrant rice, which is slightly jasmine-scented. This should first be thoroughly rinsed at least three times, then placed in a heavy saucepan with water – 450g (1lb) rice, 450ml (¾pint) water. Cover the pan and bring the contents quickly to the boil. Stir, cover again and cook for 20 minutes. Better still, use an electric rice cooker.

If you cannot find Thai fragrant rice, use any standard long-grain white rice, though this will have a bland taste compared to the jasmine-scented variety. I do not recommend any of the instant or boil-in-the-bag options, which are in any case superfluous if one has an electric rice cooker.

The other variety of rice used is sticky or glutinous rice. 450g (1lb) glutinous rice should be soaked for at least 3 hours, drained and thoroughly rinsed, then placed on muslin in the upper compartment of a steamer and steamed for 30 minutes.

One recipe (see page 186) requires black sticky rice (glutinous black rice), an unpolished rice, which is actually dark red in colour and available only from specialist shops.

**Cooking rice for a village
wedding, Malaysia**

Traditional kitchen, Thailand

Rice papers (bánh trang) are dried-off white crêpes used in Vietnamese cooking. They are round and have a cross-hatched pattern from the trays on which they are dried. They can be found in specialist shops, or in large French supermarkets, which often have a Vietnamese cookery section.

NOODLES — There are five basic noodles, all of Chinese origin, used throughout Southeast Asia:

1 Rice river noodles or rice sticks – broad, flat, white rice flour noodles, which are usually bought fresh though they are also available dried. They are sticky and the strands need to be separated before cooking.
2 Rice vermicelli – small, wiry-looking noodles, which are usually sold dried.
3 Medium flat rice flour noodles – looking rather like thin tagliatelle.
4 Egg noodles – yellow (more often from colouring than egg) noodles, which are usually spaghetti-like and curled up in 'nests' which should be shaken loose before cooking.
5 Cellophane noodles – thin, wiry, soya bean noodles, also confusingly referred to as vermicelli by some producers.

There are some noodles that are unique to a particular country and difficult to find elsewhere – fortunately the differences are very slight and I have always substituted an easy-to-buy alternative. Mien are clear Vietnamese noodles made from a mix of rice and manioc flour, but very similar to the rice vermicelli used in this book. Laksa noodles are rarely found outside Malaysia and Singapore, but they are nearly the same as the medium flat rice flour noodles used here.

Dried noodles need to be soaked in water for 20 minutes before cooking. The weights given in this book are always for either fresh or soaked noodles, not the dry weight.

Small green aubergine

Pea aubergine

Large purple/black aubergine

Round aubergine, green and yellow

Egg noodles

Cellophane noodles

Rice vermicelli

Rice river noodles

Medium flat rice flour noodles

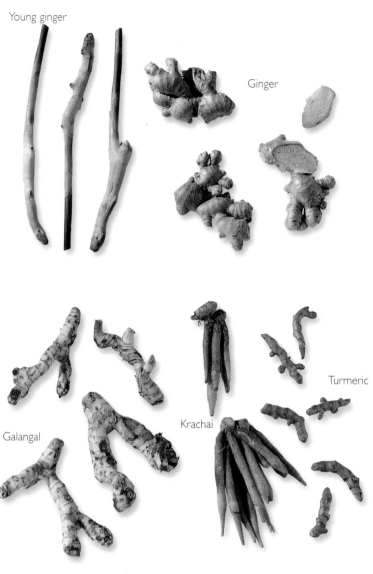

Young ginger

Ginger

Galangal

Krachai

Turmeric

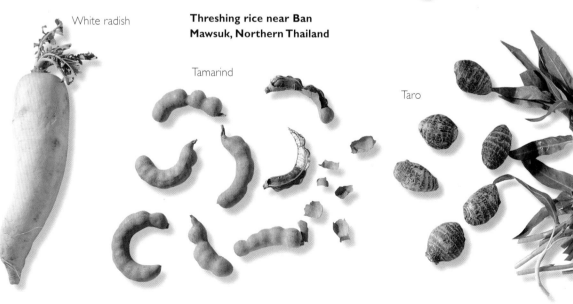

White radish

Threshing rice near Ban Mawsuk, Northern Thailand

Tamarind

Taro

Morning glory

Food market, Pagan, Burma

STOCKS – You should try to maintain a stock pot if you plan to prepare a lot of these recipes. (If you want to make something quickly, simply substitute plain water while being a little more liberal with any other flavourings required.) A good stock is essential for most of the soup recipes. Chicken, beef or pork stock should be made from the meat and bones alone, not mixed with any vegetables or herbs.

For chicken stock: cover the carcasses with water, bring to the boil, reduce the heat and simmer for at least 2 hours, skimming the surface to remove any impurities. The procedure is the same for beef and pork stock. What I call a 'rich beef stock' is made by including the edible offal – heart, liver and kidneys.

Vegetable stock needs some help – my version involves boiling up a medium-sized onion with 2 medium-sized carrots, 2 celery stalks, some coriander stems and a few whole black peppercorns. You can use anything similar, but obviously not highly flavoured or coloured vegetables like beetroot. Don't salt your stock as it may have to be reduced down and so become inedibly salty, or it may have to be used with other salty flavourings.

In all cases the liquid should have reduced by about one fifth by the end of the cooking process.

PRIMARY FLAVOURS FISH SAUCE – This is the main flavouring of Southeast Asian food, used as salt is in Western cooking. The sauce is the liquid produced when fish is fermented in salt. Once made in large earthenware jars by almost every household, it is now a mass-produced product. While each Southeast Asian country has its own brand names, the fish sauce found in the West is usually either from Thailand (nam pla) or Vietnam (nuoc mam).

There is no basic difference in quality or taste between the fish sauce of the two nations, but considerable variation between one bottle and the next, mainly depending on age. The best fish sauce is young and has a light whisky-like colour, which will indicate a refreshingly salty taste, palatable on the tongue. The worst is old, dark and bitter-tasting. You can get some indication of the colour by holding the bottle up to the light but the sauce fully reveals its true nature only when a little is poured out and tasted.

Until an accurate and supervised system of dating production is introduced there will remain an element of chance in buying fish sauce. If you find a particular brand that is satisfactory, stick to it as long as your supplier can keep it in stock.

While I have given average quantities in these recipes, you should always adjust the amount of fish sauce you use according to its saltiness. Vegetarians who do not eat fish or fish products may substitute light soy sauce, bearing in mind that it is usually less salty than fish sauce.

SOY SAUCE – Light soy sauce is thin, with a clear, delicately salty flavour and can be used as a condiment. Dark soy sauce is thicker, with a stronger, sweeter flavour, and is used mainly to colour food during the cooking process.

BEAN SAUCE – This is made from lightly mashed black or yellow fermented soya beans: the yellow is more salty, the black gives a deeper colour. It is not as frequently used as fish or soy sauce, so buy only a small jar.

OYSTER SAUCE – A thick, brown liquid, this is made from oysters cooked in soy sauce then mixed with seasonings. Surprisingly, the end-product is not fishy-tasting, but richly meaty.

PICKLED OR FERMENTED FISH – This is exactly as one would expect: pieces of fish salted and preserved to produce a very smelly, richly flavoured liquid with fish pieces. Every Southeast Asian country has its own name for it, but it is basically the same everywhere and you will definitely need to have a jar of it for many of the recipes in this book. I recommend quickly boiling a little before use in order to kill off any impurities.

SHRIMP PASTE – Not unlike Western anchovy paste, this dark purple paste has a disturbingly pungent aroma that disappears during cooking. Store it in a tightly sealed jar or risk creating a bad smell in your kitchen.

PRESERVED VEGETABLES — There are two varieties of preserved vegetables: dry pickled white radish, sometimes erroneously called 'pickled turnip', and dry pickled hard vegetable stems, usually called 'preserved vegetable'. Sold in jars, only a tiny amount of either is used to flavour a dish.

RICE VINEGAR — There is a wide range of this clear vinegar made from long-grain rice, varying from light-coloured to the older, strongly flavoured, dark-red varieties. For Southeast Asian cooking, young light vinegar is preferable and even that may be slightly diluted with water to moderate the taste. Most readily available rice vinegars will be Chinese; be careful to avoid those that contain monosodium glutamate or any other seasonings.

PICKLED GARLIC — Whole heads of garlic are preserved in a rich salty liquid for use as a powerful flavouring. Always buy these ready-made.

PICKLED CABBAGE — This you will need to make yourself. It can be used as an ingredient or served as an accompaniment. Chop 450g (1lb) firm white cabbage (ideally Swatow mustard cabbage) into 5cm (2in) square pieces and leave for 24 hours to wilt. Place in a preserving jar and cover with 225ml (8fl oz) rice vinegar boiled with 115g (4oz) sugar and 1 tablespoon salt (the mixture should be cooled before placing in the jar). Seal the jar firmly and leave for 3 days before use (there is no need to refrigerate).

Fish, Khon Kaen market, Thailand

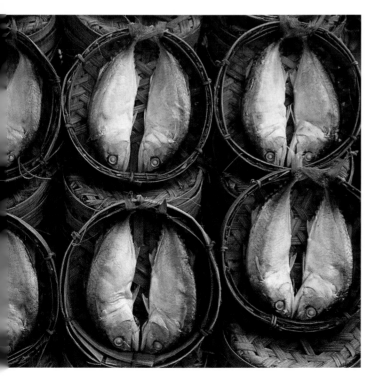

HOT FLAVOURS CHILLIES — There are some 300 varieties of the capsicum family and 10 are used in Thai cooking alone. However, only 5 are common to Southeast Asian cuisine and are listed here. Chillies are sub-divided primarily by length, and only a few have commonly understood names, which makes identification difficult. As Thai cooking and Thai ingredients are becoming standard in Western countries, I have given the Thai names in brackets, as these are the only ones which are likely to be of any use.

1 Birdseye chillies (prik khee noo suan): tiny, about 1cm (½in) long, red or green, intensely hot, these chillies do not keep well and importers tend to prefer the next size up, which is probably all that you will find. However, the birdseye chilli is the one most often used in the region, both cooked and raw in sauces.
2 Small red or green chillies (prik khee noo): about 2.5cm (1in) long, only slightly less hot than birdseye chillies, these are the most frequently recommended variety for the recipes in this book. If, however, you do manage to find birdseye chillies and you are a hot food fanatic, use them instead.
3 Medium chillies (cayenne peppers, prik chee faa): finger-length, up to 7.5–10cm (3–4in) long. Red or green, these are slightly less hot than the small varieties and are used for making chilli powder.
4 Large chillies (prik yuak): light green to red, these are similar to the sweet pepper though thinner and closest to the Hungarian white paprika which would be an acceptable substitute. They are used as a vegetable, fried or stuffed.
5 Large dried red chillies (prik haeng): these sun-dried chillies are deep maroon/red and about 7.5–10cm (3–4in) long. They are hotter than medium chillies but slightly less hot than birdseye or small red/green chillies.
Note: chilli sauce is a dipping sauce, not a cooking ingredient, and is made from a mix of hot and sweet chillies.

DRY SPICES — Like the chilli, these are not indigenous to the region but were brought to the coastal areas chiefly by Indian traders, promptly transforming the cooking wherever they appeared. They are mainly pounded to form pastes for making the stew-like curries that are quite different from the thick varieties found in modern India. The dry spices used in Southeast Asia are cloves, coriander seeds, cumin, cinnamon, star anise, nutmeg and cardamom. We also use five-spice powder, a ground mixture of peppercorns, fennel, cloves, cinnamon and star anise.

Some recipes require ready-made curry powder; the variety most used in the region corresponds to the mild yellow Madras curry powder, which contains coriander, turmeric, mustard seeds, Bengal gram, cumin, chillies, fennel, pepper, garlic and salt.

HERBS — Away from the coast, cooks rely less on dry spices and more on the herbs and herb seeds that were originally used to flavour Southeast Asian food. The principal herbs used are:

Market, central Thailand

BASIL – Two varieties are used: sweet basil and holy basil. Sweet basil (*Ocimum basilicum*, Asian sweet basil, cinnamon basil) has shiny green leaves tinged with purple, and its smell has just a hint of cinnamon and clove. It is generally cooked at the last moment or used as a garnish. Holy basil (*O. sanctum*) has narrower, slightly hairy leaves, with a more noticeable, reddish-purple tinge. Its taste is much stronger and it must be cooked to release the flavour. Both varieties can be used dried, but in this form have a slightly musty flavour.

CORIANDER (*Coriandrum sativum*, cilantro, Chinese parsley) – A member of the parsley family (it most resembles Italian or flat-leaf parsley) whose leaves are also used mainly as a garnish. Coriander roots, along with the base of the stalks, are much used in Thai cooking. They are crushed with garlic and pepper to make a marinade for meat and fish. The roots and stalks can be deep-frozen successfully.

KAFFIR LIME (Citrus hystrix, wild lime) – The fruit is knobbly with little juice, skin or zest but its used as a strong citrus flavouring, as are the hard, dark green leaves that grow in pairs from the twig-like stems. There is a possibility that the EC may ban imports of kaffir lime fruit and leaves to prevent disease blighting European lime trees. In this event, the only (though inadequate) alternative would be to use dried leaves, assuming that these escape the ban, or to add a little amount of squeezed European lime juice towards the end of the cooking process.

LEMON GRASS (*Cymbopogon citratus*) – This is really a plant, a variety of hard grass, but is used as a herb for its refreshing lemon/mint flavour. The pale green, almost white, bulbous stalk looks like a fat spring onion. You need to peel away the hard outer layer, but even then only tiny rings of the plant will cook sufficiently to be edible. Larger sections are useful only for flavouring and should be removed before the dish is eaten. When cooked, the flavour remains lemony but loses any unpleasant trace of acidity and acquires a slight gingery note. Chopped lemon grass rings can be deep-frozen and used without defrosting.

MINT (*Mentha* spp.) – The mint used extensively in Vietnamese cooking and which has spread around the region is Vietnamese mint (*Polygonum* spp.). This has a slight flavour of coriander and is either tossed into a dish at the last moment or eaten raw, but it is never cooked as its flavour would dominate any dish. This is unlikely to be available outside Southeast Asia and the best substitute

spearmint (*M. spicata*), with its long, oval, greyish-green leaves, as these have a stronger flavour than garden mint.

RHIZOMES These are not roots, as is often assumed, but stems that grow underground. Four types of rhizome are used in Southeast Asian cooking, each offering a slightly different ginger flavour. They look somewhat similar and are used in the same way: generally a small length is cut off the knobbly stem, then slivered quite finely to release its flavours during cooking.

GINGER (*Zingiber officinale*, green ginger, root ginger or ginger root) – Resembling knobbly, golden-beige, bulbous fingers, root ginger in the West is too often old, dry and stringy, unlike Asian ginger which is always young, tender and juicy. Asian ginger gives the basic 'straight' ginger taste that clears the head and adds a slight yet sharp sweetness.

GALANGAL (*Languas galanga* alt, *Alpinia galanga*, galingale, Thai or Siamese ginger, greater galangal) – With thinner, smoother fingers, this is cream-coloured with pink tips. Slightly harder than ginger, its flavour, while 'gingery', has a distinctively hot, peppery edge that makes it especially suitable for curries.

KRACHAI (*Boesenbergia pandurate.* alt. *Kaempferia pandurate*, Chinese keys, sometimes incorrectly called lesser galangal or lesser ginger) – Consisting of thin, light brown cylinders in a cluster, said to resemble a bunch of keys, hence its name. This gives a ginger/lemon flavour that is especially suitable with fish dishes or to give a citrus tang to soups.

TURMERIC (*Curcuma domestica*) – Brown, rather flaky on the outside, it is the rich orange-yellow beneath that is most important. The warm spicy taste is a useful addition, but turmeric is often used simply because of the bright colour it gives any dish. It is the source of the somewhat lurid hue of the Anglo-Indian piccalilli and in many parts of Asia it is used as much as a dye as a cooking ingredient. In the past, it was only available ground, and in this form can be slightly musty. Today, fresh turmeric is more easily available in the West. Buy only small amounts of the ground variety as its quickly loses it flavour.

UNFAMILIAR VEGETABLES AUBERGINE (eggplant) – While the large purple-black aubergine common in the West is used in Southeast Asian cooking, we also use the tiny hard pea aubergine and the round green aubergine, roughly 2.5cm (1in) in diameter, which are quite different. Their smallness and hardness make them especially good ingredients for boiled dishes like Thai or Laotian curries, in which they will remain al dente.

LONGBEAN (long-podded cowpea, yard-long bean, snakebean) – Imagine a French bean which is slightly thicker and up to 1m (3ft) long. Choose darker rather than lighter coloured beans.

MORNING GLORY (water spinach, swamp cabbage, swamp spinach, water convolvulus) – The long jointed stems of this plant stay firm when cooked, while the leaves become limp and the flavour is similar to that of Western spinach. It is a difficult vegetable to keep as the leaves quickly yellow and go bad.

Traditional cheroots, Burma

TAMARIND – Pulp extracted from the brittle pod of the tamarind tree is used, most often dissolved in water as tamarind water or tamarind juice, to impart a pungent, sour, lemony flavour that gives a tremendous lift to any dish. It is a principal ingredient of Worcestershire sauce. Compressed blocks of the pulp can be bought in Indian stores. A poor substitute is double the amount of lemon juice, but use this only if it is impossible to find tamarind.

TARO – This is a rather bland tuber used as a vegetable or, mixed with flavourings, as a dessert.

WHITE RADISH (mooli, giant white radish, daikon) – This root vegetable can be served raw as a salad vegetable or cooked, whereupon it loses its cool sharpness and becomes somewhat like turnip in flavour.

OTHER UNUSUAL INGREDIENTS AGAR AGAR – This powder, made from seaweed, is sold in Asian stores and used as a gelling agent to make jellies, both sweet and savoury, without the need to refrigerate the liquid. It is suitable for vegetarians.

BANANA LEAVES – The leaves of the banana tree are used to wrap ingredients for grilling or steaming. The leaves help retain liquid and add a slight flavour to the dish. They are now available in Oriental stores in the West, though unfortunately you will have to buy rather a large packet, probably more than you will need.

BEANCURD (tofu) – Blocks of white fresh beancurd, made from curdled extract of yellow soya beans, are usually sold in plastic trays in a little of their own liquid. These should be used on the day of purchase, but can be kept for three days providing the liquid is poured away and replaced with a little fresh water each day. Cubes of fresh beancurd can be deep-fried until golden brown; these are fresher and creamier than the ready-fried beancurd on sale in Chinese stores. Beancurd sheets, sold dried in packets, look like wrinkled brown paper and need to be soaked for 5–6 minutes before use. When wet, any torn sections can be patched together with ease. Red beancurd, sold in jars, is pickled or fermented beancurd. Its strong flavour is used for sauces.

COCONUT – The fresh white meat of the newly ripe coconut is much used in curries and desserts in coastal areas, where the coconut palm is common. It is the coconut milk and cream, however, that are essential to many Southeast Asian recipes. These are made by soaking and pressing the grated coconut meat: a first pressing produces the thick cream, a second the thinner milk. Canned coconut cream is perfectly acceptable; if milk is required, open the can, let the contents settle then pour off the thinner liquid at the top; otherwise stir well and use the full cream.

Young monks in the pagoda on Mandalay Hill, Burma

Elephants, northern Thailand

FISH BALLS – These small round dumplings made from fish and flour may be bought in Chinese stores and are used as a cooking ingredient, nearly always with noodles.

BLACK BEANS – These are just that, black beans, sold under that name in Chinese stores. In truth, these particular beans are mainly selected for their colour and could be replaced with almost any firm small bean, whether red, white or whatever. You can buy black beans in vacuum packs and they can be kept for a very long time in a well-sealed preserving jar, in a cool dark place.

MUSHROOMS – The mushroom most used in Asian cooking is the black fungus mushroom (cloud ear or *champignon noir*), usually bought dried and then soaked for 20–30 minutes at room temperature. Take care to remove any sandy grit and tough stalks. The smaller mushrooms are better. Dried Chinese mushrooms (shiitake) are the same size and shape, though slightly smaller than the common Western large flat mushroom. If no particular variety of mushroom is specified, any commonly available edible fungus will do: e.g. *champignon*, button mushroom, large flat mushroom (parasol), oyster mushroom (*pleurote*), straw mushroom.

PALM SUGAR – This is produced from the sap of the coconut palm and has a rich caramel flavour quite different from that of cane sugar. The best is soft and brown in colour, with a toffee-like aroma. It is sold in Asian stores, preferably in well-compressed cakes that are easy to keep. You could substitute a dark Demerara sugar but it will not have quite the same distinctive taste.

PRESERVED PLUM – This Chinese fruit, like a cross between a plum, an apricot and an olive, preserved in salted rice vinegar, has a very strong sweet taste with pleasing sour undertones. Scrapings of the flesh are used to make plum sauce. Jars of preserved plums are always available in Chinese stores.

Thailand

EATEN BY FISH

Every Friday evening, the domestic terminal at Bangkok's Don Muang Airport is the setting for a frantic spectacle, as hordes of Bangkokians, often entire families, hurry to catch flights out to their weekend homes — up in the northern mountains, down on the southern beaches, anywhere away from the eye-stinging, lung-clogging pollution of Southeast Asia's fastest-growing metropolitan nightmare. Yet only a generation ago no one would have believed that such a thing might ever be possible. When I was a schoolboy in Bangkok in the late fifties, Thailand was a country little visited even by its own people. Poor roads and limited transportation made travel arduous, with the result that the regions beyond the capital and the central area of the country seemed to us as remote as foreign lands.

Royal ploughing ceremony, Bangkok

In those days it was possible to divide the kingdom into four distinct regions — the Centre, the North, the Northeast and the South. Of these, there were only two places with which we were familiar. One was the historic walled city of Chiang Mai, the northern capital, which could be reached by the old, slow, overnight train that chugged its way right up the centre of Thailand, to what seemed to us a magical place of mountains and forests and rapturously cool air after the tropical heat of Bangkok. Our other adventure was a journey south, around the western shore of the Gulf of Thailand, to the little fishing village of Hua Hin, where the royal family had a villa, making it a fashionable place for seaside holidays. The sense of isolation and strangeness these places then had meant that any cultural differences were very apparent. People in the north looked different, they wore different costumes, lived in different sorts of villages and, above all, they ate different things. This was the biggest thrill of all, for on the rare occasions when we did travel, we were regaled with things to eat that were as exotic to us as our Bangkok food would have been to someone in Britain and America, had they ever had a chance to eat it, which in those days was highly unlikely.

In the central area of the country, the food we ate was a product of the rivers and canals that crossed the great emerald plains — rice above all, but also lots of freshwater fish, with sea fish from the nearby Gulf of Thailand. Agriculturally, this was the most productive area of the country: every house had its vegetable plot; village markets were piled high with aubergines, long beans, morning glory (water spinach), cabbages, tomatoes; and there was no shortage of flavourings — sour limes and tangy lemon grass, sweet ginger and galangal, savoury fish sauce and shrimp paste, and the fermented fish that smells so off-putting yet tastes so good once the cooking process has worked its magic. Meals in the central area were short on meat, but long on vegetables, fish, and hot and spicy dips balanced by creamy coconut dishes. Apart from feast days when there would be a huge communal cook-in, village food was delicious but modest. There was always a mountain of rice, but perhaps helped down by no more than a very spicy dip accompanied by some small deep-fried river fish with a dish of spiced vegetable, say morning glory or long beans.

Such spicy dips or nam prik, literally 'chilli water', began as a peasant staple but are now classics of Thai cuisine. The taste of these dips is often too hot and too rich in fermented flavours for newcomers to our food. After a time, however, most come to appreciate the subtle qualities that these tiny bowls of mixed tastes and textures can offer. Peasant food it may once have been, but the grandest Bangkok ladies struggle to prepare their own special versions. In the days when we had servants to prepare our meals, my mother would devote herself to making her particular nam prik, pounding the ingredients in a mortar and carefully blending the fish sauce with any crisp vegetables that her particular recipe might require. My Aunt Chinda, who is a senior banker in Bangkok, likes to prepare her version: Nam Prik Gung Pow, the recipe for which I've given in this chapter (page 48), which she makes with fresh prawns whenever she entertains colleagues or clients. The dip itself may be small, but the accompaniments can be highly decorative — fans of deep-fried fish, heaps of crisp raw vegetables: cucumber and pea-aubergines, or lightly blanched stems like morning glory, along with squares of cold omelette. The flavour of the 'water' should be a balance of sweet and savoury, ranging from outright sugariness to the tang of fish and seafood, with each specialist emphasizing their particular preference – my mother's version was always quite salty, whereas my aunt prefers sweetness.

You can find versions of nam prik all over Thailand, and back in my schooldays there were distinct regional variations. In the North, the big difference was that it was always served with glutinous rice. A woven basket of the sticky grains was there for every meal and the great treat was a kantoke dinner, where diners sat on the ground at a raised round table, like a tray, with a selection of dishes, say a spicy nam prik dip served with crispy deep-fried pork skin, a curry, and certainly a laab, a spicy dish with highly flavoured minced meat, balanced by cool crispy salad leaves. At a kantoke dinner you ate with your fingers, making little balls of sticky rice to help lift other food to your mouth.

In those days, the North was certainly different. It was only in 1927 that King Rama VII became the first Thai monarch to visit his Northern capital, riding into Chiang Mai on an elephant borrowed from the British Consul. Until recently the city remained a small, antiquated backwater, with sumptuous temples and a glorious market, famous for its stunning array of pickles and preserves. As this was the region of mountains and forests, with village huts set in small clearings rather than out on the open rice fields, much of the food was from the wild – the result of hunting and gathering, rather than cultivation. Meals seemed more solid, with more meat – wild game, such as deer and even buffalo, flavoured with wild herbs or dawn-picked mushrooms, and everything sharper-tasting because the food was prepared without the leavening effect of coconut milk or the sweetness of palm sugar, the coconut palms being mainly confined to southern parts of Thailand.

A dish like Jin Ping (page 35) shows clearly this difference – jin is the northern word for pig or pork and jin ping is a sort of northern satay, with the marinated meat being grilled on skewers. Instead of being served with the usual peanut-and-coconut-milk sauce, however, in the North it comes with a fiery dip of chilli and lime juice – an altogether different set of tastes and textures. Indeed, we loved Northern food on the rare occasions when we could get it, precisely because of those powerful tastes and because there were products that were then unobtainable in Bangkok. When you took the train back to the capital you could see most of your fellow passengers buying special northern sausage from hawkers on the platform as presents for family and

Spectacular limestone outcrops rise out of Phangna Bay, southern Thailand

friends, usually eaten as an appetizer with nibbles of chopped shallot, raw ginger, salted peanuts and coriander leaves.

While we did visit Chiang Mai occasionally, any farther north – as far as the town of Chiang Rai – was out of the question. And beyond, high in the Golden Triangle, the mountainous region that Thailand shares with Burma and Laos, was the world of the Hill Tribes, people ethnically and culturally different from us, living isolated lives in remote villages, much as they had for centuries, barely affected by modern life. When I was an art student in Bangkok the little I knew of these strange people I learned from a friend, Yod Chai, who came from Chiang Rai, and who was one of the few at that time to appreciate the highly coloured and decorated woven cloths and heavy silverware jewellery that the tribespeople wore. Yod Chai means 'Top Man' and, at a time when the rest of us were hung up on Western fashions – crazy about the Beatles and longing to visit London and New York – he was way ahead in loving natural materials, wood and dried leaves, plain earth colours and handmade objects. Whenever he went home to Chiang Rai, Yod Chai would bring us Hill Tribe woven bags, black and red waistcoats, and the round pom-pom hats that they wore, and would regale us with stories of their strange dances in a misty world of opium poppies and fierce warlords, stories that didn't sound quite real, more like ancient folk tales.

As for the Northeast, that was definitely a closed book. Indeed everyone in Bangkok did their best to avoid going there. Issan, as we call that huge region, was a notorious punishment post for civil servants and soldiers, a strange forbidding place of droughts and floods, of famine and neglect. Its people were not Thai as we were, but Lao, ethnically the same as the people living across the Mekong in the neighbouring Kingdom of Laos, as it then was. Of course, we knew what the Issan people were like, as thousands of them were obliged to migrate south in search of work, but their food was a rare pleasure only occasionally found on food stalls in Bangkok. Some years back an Issan woman set up a stall in our soi, or lane, offering what we always called Issan chicken, which was a half chicken, flattened out, marinated and barbecued, and often served with som tam, the highly charged, chilli-strong salad of grated raw papaya flavoured with chilli, fish sauce and ground peanuts, that was the one Issan dish you could find everywhere. What I didn't know at the time was that this fiery flavour was typical of a region where any food product was usually in short supply. With little meat and few vegetables, what there was needed to be highly spiced in order to help consume lots of rice – again sticky rice – in order to feed a family with limited resources. This meagre regime had to be augmented with whatever was available: frogs and insects – anything nutritious in fact.

The South, the narrow isthmus leading down to Malaysia, was different again. If anything, the land beyond our seaside holiday village of Hua Hin was even more remote than Issan. We were told that this was a place of bandits and danger – even the little old train from Bangkok to Singapore was thought to be unsafe. By

Winowing rice

Transplanting rice

reputation, the South was a languid sort of place, with palm-fringed islands, unspoiled because unvisited, and certainly with fascinating food. We knew about the Mussaman curry – an exotic delight in Bangkok, its rich dry spice flavours and the use of the man farang, the 'foreign potato', both imported from Malaysia (hence the name Mussaman which means Muslim). The extreme South was the land of mosques and veiled women, and much richer, darker tastes, the result of the spice trade with India and the Arabic connections that came with Islam.

There ought, however, to have been a fifth region, as far as food was concerned – Bangkok itself, for it was obvious that the one place in the country that had any claims to a cosmopolitan life would have a far broader range of culinary styles. Since the days of Ayuthaya, the old capital of Siam, that was destroyed during a Burmese invasion in the late 18th century, a form of cooking has grown up that is far more complex than the simple fare found in the countryside. Originally developed for the Royal Court and the palaces of the Thai nobility, this complex cuisine consisted of successions of small delicacies, decorated with intricately carved fruit and vegetables transformed into fragile flowers, with exquisite flavours and unusual ingredients. These creations were treated with the same respect as the highly stylized performances of Thai classical dance that are considered the summit of Thai culture. This sophisticated food was in turn influenced by outside ideas, especially from China, brought by visiting merchants or by the waves of Chinese immigrants who settled and became the country's principal commercial community. At the same time, Indian traders brought dry spices and even the Portuguese played a part, bringing the chilli, originally from South America, which more than any other single element transformed Thai cooking and, on a lesser scale, the practice of cooking sweet dishes with eggs.

After the departure of the Burmese and the establishment of a new dynasty at the new capital of Khrung Thep, or Bangkok as visitors called it, elements of this once exclusive cuisine began to spread into the homes of the rich and well-placed, and when I was young even moderately well-off families with servants to help them enjoyed a standard of cooking that seems quite astonishing in retrospect.

Our evening meal – taken early, at about 6.30 – was quite an affair. Everyone bathed and changed into light clothes, say a loose cotton shirt and Chinese-style wraparound silk 'pyjama' trousers, while our main cook Khun Aat sat cross-legged in the smoky outhouse, cooking over a charcoal stove, as the younger girls, who normally minded the children or coped with the ironing, ran about fetching and carrying for her. Mother might be preparing her special nam prik in the modern 'show' kitchen inside the house, while father sat at the table drinking whisky and sampling hotter dishes that were brought out as they were cooked and which served as appetizers. Gradually the range of courses would build up on the table – a selection intended to balance flavours, textures and heat – mother's spicy dip and a light soup to balance it, a curry such as Gaeng Kiow Wan Nua (Beef in Green Curry with Coconut, see page 40), always a special favourite, perhaps further counterbalanced by a sweeter dish. Ideally, there would also be a vegetable dish and some sort of fish or seafood.

When all was served, the cry of 'Kin kow' or 'Eat rice', the classic call to food, would summon me and my four brothers to table with father, while my mother and sister supervised the ladling out of a fairly large mountain of rice for each of us. From then on everything was shared, with each taking just a little of whatever dish we wanted with our own spoons, carrying it back to eat with the rice. We always ate with forks and spoons – chopsticks were Chinese and only for noodles – and we never heaped lots of different things on our plates at the same time – just a little bit of this, then that, taking it easy, letting it digest, as we talked and laughed about the shared news of the day. We always finished our rice, after which there would be fresh fruit – mangoes, rose apples, star fruit, whatever was in season. Occasionally, there was also a sweet pudding: either 'dry', like Kow Niew Tat (Sweet Sticky Rice Cakes, see page 47), or 'wet', like Kai Wan (Sweet Ginger Eggs, see page 48).

Eating out was a different matter – on important occasions we nearly always went to a Chinese restaurant, where a many-course feast would be consumed at a large round table with a revolving centre. There were some long-established Thai restaurants – like Vichit in the old government district near Democracy Monument, where civil servants liked to lunch – but for something special it was grand Chinese cooking that we preferred. Out of the home, Thai food was fast food – lunches and snacks, grabbed at one of the countless stalls that turned many side streets and market areas into open-air restaurants, or taken from passing food-hawkers whose pedal-wagons roamed the back streets of the capital, offering everything from fried rice to desserts and ices, in a continuously revolving circuit. If I went jogging early in the morning in nearby Lumpini Park, I could pick up some tou hou tod (deep-fried beancurd in a sweet sauce) for my breakfast, or sit at the morning food market over a bowl of Kow Tom Het (Rice Soup with Mushrooms, see page 41), flavoured with garlic and ginger. Other than that, Thai food was something eaten at home, and at that time it was totally unknown in the West.

All that changed with the war in Vietnam and the decision by the Americans to help our modest backwater kingdom protect itself from communism. As part of this scheme, Bangkok was made

Drying fish near Krabi, southern Thailand

Bangkok's notorious traffic

the principal rest and recreation centre for the GIs fighting in that tragic conflict. The result was two-fold: a massive investment in the infrastructure of the country, with new facilities for aircraft and with highways ploughing north to the Mekong, while at the same time hotels were opened around the country as visitors began to flood in, bringing with them the inevitable mix of good and bad. On the one hand, the country was opened up to undreamed-of outside influences, transforming the economy and providing paid work for tens of thousands who had previously been tied to the land. At the same time whole areas of our main cities were changed into red-light districts, exaggerating the exodus from the poorer regions, where the effects of this capitalist revolution were last to arrive.

Nothing was untouched by this whirlwind, not even our food. The original GIs may have wanted hamburgers and hot-dogs, but some were adventurous enough to sit at street-side stalls where they learned to like Thai food. If there was one dish alone which converted the world to Thai cooking it would have to be Pad Thai (see page 47), the noodle dish whose mixture of flavours and textures is quite different from Chinese cooking, blending dried chilli, pounded nuts, raw spring onion, lime and fish sauce, along with whatever main ingredient the diner chooses – from pork to prawns. This is the fast food of Thailand and many visitors soon come to prefer it to a Big Mac.

Despite the disruptive side effects, the American presence stimulated the economic boom that has made Thailand one of the new tiger economies of Asia. It began with factories assembling

Japanese products, using our cheap labour. A few years back there was a hugely popular hit song that satirized this process; the singer pointing out that, while everything he bought was supposed to be Japanese, whenever he looked at the back it said 'Made in Thailand'. That was, of course, just a stage on the road to development, and today goods really are made in the Kingdom, though with the result that anyone who has recently visited Bangkok can reveal – the 'Venice of the East', a magical place of meandering canals, with a tree-line broken only by the golden stupas of the many temples and the gilded spires of the Royal Palace, has gone. Khrung Thep, the 'City of Angels', as we have always called it, has now overtaken its distant namesake Los Angeles in sprawl and pollution.

Our family house, which once stood peacefully in its own grounds at the centre of the business district, is now hemmed in by soaring skyscrapers. As I write, a new one is currently going up on the plot next door and, recently, after a bag of builder's tools came crashing through our roof, the construction company agreed to evacuate my parents to a nearby apartment block until work is completed. It is a kind of madness. It is almost impossible to get about by foot any more, and some of my friends need three hours to get to work through the near rock-solid traffic jams. One lawyer I know is driven to his office in a campervan, while he reclines on a bed at the back watching videos!

Traditional pottery

Nothing has remained unchanged. As the Vietnamese War receded and the GIs left, tourists began to take their place, and over 20 years this has developed into a boom industry, with ever larger hotels offering a mix of Western and Thai food. In the main centres, Thai restaurants opened on an unprecedented scale, with servants deserting the houses of the rich to find work as chefs, preparing the same variety of dishes, beautifully decorated with carved fruit and vegetables, the sort of fine dining that only the very wealthy and well-born had known before. And this cuisine has now adapted to Western dining habits, with different courses, along with appetizers, and special food for buffets. Whatever was needed, Thai food could fit the bill; because, unlike other 'local' cuisines, that had only a limited number of traditional practices, Thai cooking was already a broad international cuisine which had absorbed many influences, from India, China and its nearer neighbours, and could absorb many more. Like the French and the Chinese, we Thai have a major 'international' cuisine, rather than a local one, which, in retrospect, makes its spread outwards into other continents seem less astonishing than it did at the time.

Of course, it was inevitable that, once they returned home, the huge surge of tourists from Western Europe and America would wish to sample again the food that they had enjoyed on holiday. The result has been the extraordinary explosion of Thai restaurants around the world. When I first came to London as a student in 1976 there were, at most, four Thai restaurants in the entire United Kingdom, trying to serve some semblance of Thai food without having access to all the necessary ingredients. When I recently helped found the Thai Restaurants Association in London we couldn't count the number of potential members. As for ingredients you can get most of what you need – from curry pastes to fresh lemon grass – at almost any local supermarket.

Much of the food offered in overseas Thai restaurants is basic Bangkok cooking mixed with the sort of Chinese dishes popular with Thai people. When I opened my first restaurant in London, The Chiang Mai, in 1981, I was determined to offer something a little more authentic, with a menu that included dishes from the North. Ten years later, when I helped launch the Chiang Rai in Manchester, we went even further and my latest effort, the Thai Bistro in Chiswick, West London, has a changing menu that offers a choice of food from every part of the country.

All this reflects what has been happening in Thailand since the economic boom opened up the country to its own citizens. Over the past 20 years I have tried to visit every part of my native land, enjoying its cultural treasures and sampling its local foods. With Thai Airways now covering the entire country, nowhere is off-limits any more. Many Bangkokians have beachside villas along the Western Gulf, while others fly to weekend cottages in the North. My banker Aunt and some of her friends have even developed a country estate in the mountains near Chiang Rai, and when I went to visit I seized the opportunity to look up my old friend Yod Chai, who had gone back to his home town after he finished his studies. I wasn't surprised to find that he'd opened a gallery-cum-shop, 'Silver Birch', at 891 Phaholyotin, the town's main thoroughfare, and that it is filled with the most amazing hand-crafted objects – tiny carved figures that move when you pull strings, hanging mobiles of fish and dragon-flies, tiny hand-beaten silver spoons with peanut shell handles. And the Top Man isn't alone: a thriving artists' colony has grown up in a place free from the stress and pollution of the capital, where people can still live close to nature. Yod Chai took me to the 'art village' created by his friend: Tuan Dachanee, now one of Thailand's leading artists, who has put together a compound of traditional northern buildings, all painted a deep black and decorated with animal skulls and bulls' horns, which gives the place an air of an American-Indian compound. Khun Dachanee himself always wears the same deep black and creates mysterious monochrome paintings of figures, half-human, half-animal, which he tends to give away to those he considers truly like them, while spurning offers from those he considers to be merely rich. His village, Nang Laer, is open to all, and if its creator is not away at one of his other studios in Europe, America or Japan, he will always take time to come and talk with anyone who wants to know more about his ideas.

Despite all the frantic development that has taken place, it is still just possible to search out such havens of tranquillity, away from the skyscrapers and the freeways, though this is becoming ever harder in the South, which more than any other region has borne the brunt of the unending tourist boom. Today, the remotest islands have beach resorts, and if you want to relax in peace you have to keep one step ahead of the developers. My last discovery was Krabi province on the eastern side of the southern isthmus, overlooking the Bay of Phangna, that strange stretch of water dotted with the awesome karst outcrops that rise sheer out of the waves, weird pillars of limestone that have survived where the surrounding rocks eroded away to leave only these towering peaks topped with a fuzz of vegetation.

Most of the people who make boat tours round Phangna come on a day trip from the holiday island of Phuket, which is probably the most famous tourist spot in Thailand. When I first visited Phuket, you rented a hut on the beach and fishermen came round to offer you their catch, which you could cook on an open fire. Today it would be hard to find a square metre of sand without a towel on it; which is why I wanted to look at Krabi, which is about to open an international airport but was then still 'underdeveloped' in the best sense. Someone suggested Ao Nang beach and, when I paid off the taxi, it seemed to be everything I could wish – a long stretch of empty sand overhung with twisted palms, water you could see through, and out in the bay one of the highest

karst outcrops in the region. The dream diminished when I saw the first hotel, a three-storey affair on the wrong side of the road away from the beach, but I decided to let fate take over and walked along the coast road, past beachside restaurants, enjoying the view and longing to get into my swimming things. Suddenly I stumbled on a vision from the past – well, almost – a resort, right on the beach, with individual wooden chalets – too smart really to be huts – set among the palms. Krabi Resort turned out to be the ideal compromise between modernity and those long-lost days of sleeping on a beach mat and cooking under the stars. That afternoon I shared a boat with an Australian couple who wanted to go snorkelling under the limestone outcrop. This really was heaven, with shoals of wildly coloured, tiny fish moving about us, some of them nibbling at our hands and feet – it was nothing serious, since they were much too small for that, but just a curious tickling sensation from dozens of miniature fish mouths trying to gobble up their dinner, us!

Khun Chuan, the owner of the resort, is a local businessman and politician who wants to keep the place the way it is, even after

Royal barge crossing the Chao Phraya river to the Temple of the Dawn

the airport opens and the crowds arrive. All the local people have agreed that no high-rise blocks will be built near the sea and that any buildings will be carefully integrated into the natural setting. I wish him well, though I'm glad I got there first, especially for the food, which was southern cooking at its best. The resort has its own Yam Krabi (see page 38), a salad with mixed seafood – squid, prawns, mussels, baby clams, in a hot sauce of chilli and lime, eased with fresh pineapple and crushed peanuts; and serves classic southern recipes like pork skin with aubergine and krachai, and the famous Yellow Curry Fish (see page 43) that is now eaten all over the country.

That, of course, is the main result of this opening-up of our country – not only do we now travel out to sample the good things once exclusively found in faraway places, but these same things are now part of basic Thai cooking. Our food is much broader and more varied than it was 20 years ago. Today you can buy Chiang Mai sausage in the food halls of any of Bangkok's leading department stores, and even the food of the once despised Northeast now has its devotees. Just off the busy Sukhumvit Road, the central residential area in Soi 36, is Bahn Lao which, as its name 'Lao House' implies, is set up as an authentic Issan stilt-house, with bamboo tables and chairs outside under woven awnings. There is the jovial atmosphere of a village party, with a folk orchestra playing traditional music and food so authentic even I have to be careful, making sure I eat plenty of sticky rice with the dishes like Tom Yam Gai (Chicken and Lemon Grass Soup, see page 32) which is heavy with the rich tastes of grilled garlic, shallots and a great deal of chilli – delicious but dangerous. The place is so pretty, with masses of plants in earthenware pots and patterned walkways made of earthenware tiles, that I strongly suspect the owner must be another of those northern artists.

There is a close connection between art and food in Thailand, especially when you come to the one section of our cuisine that is still virtually unknown outside the capital, and even there only to a select few – the highly refined Royal cuisine. I had one recent experience of this, thanks to my old friend Pan who took me to Genisha, a small discreet place at Sukhumvit Soi 11, near the Ambassador Hotel. Pan was a student of art history, specializing in Thai textiles, but has been many things since – model, antique dealer and, most recently, an organizer of grand receptions, including formal dinners at the Chitralada Palace for the King and Queen. Pan's knowledge of traditional costumes means that he can arrange banquets with all the serving people dressed as if for a celebration in the ancient city of Sukhothai, and he keeps in close touch with a whole range of highly skilled craftspeople who can quickly produce the breathtaking effects he needs. He has one group who can make a vast carpet of flowers in a day, so that the King and Queen and their guests can walk on a sea of sweet-smelling colour.

Craftsmen regilding the Phra Si Ratana Chedi, near the Grand Palace, Bangkok

Dried prawns in a southern market

However, the most important element at any royal meal has to be the fantastically decorated food, for which Pan works in close contact with the Ton Kruan, the title given to the supervisor of the Royal kitchens. The present Ton Kruan is the mother of Kuhn Montri, the owner of the Genisha, where he serves the same kind of delicate food created in the palace kitchens – the reason Pan took me there. Everything we were offered depended on what was in season like the hot and sour salad made out of crab-apple blossoms, laid on the plate as if you were meant to paint it rather than eat it and the tiny balls of meat carefully wrapped in fine noodles, with just a hint of a savoury stuffing. I've given an example of this sort of elaborate delicacy: Gratong Mee Krob (see page 36), a sweet crispy noodle mixture in tiny batter baskets, a recipe to test any cook's patience! And my recipe for Tod Man Gung (Deep-fried Prawn and Sweetcorn Cakes, see page 44) is just the sort of unusual mixing of flavours expected by the Genisha's customers, some of them members of the Royal Family.

To eat this sort of food is to leave reality behind for a moment, so it is a rude shock to step out of the restaurant back into the polluted hell of Bangkok's endless traffic, the worst effect of our mad roller-coaster ride from Third World status to economic giant. While many of the results have been appalling, our food seems to have gone from strength to strength, a sign that for all our rush for growth we have not yet lost our belief that life should be sanuk, that it should be fun. The task now is to put right those areas of life that have been badly damaged by the stampede for growth, and to pray that those neighbouring countries which are about to start down this same path will learn from our mistakes and be more careful of those precious things that are so easily lost.

GAM POO OP
CRAB CLAWS WITH SPICY DIP

INGREDIENTS
- 450g (1lb) crab claws
- 2 tablespoons oil
- 2 tablespoons light soy sauce
- ½ teaspoon salt
- 1 tablespoon finely chopped garlic
- ½ teaspoon ground black pepper
- 3 sprigs of coriander, leaf and stem, chopped

FOR THE SPICY DIP:
- 4–5 small fresh red or green chillies
- 2 garlic cloves
- ¼ teaspoon salt
- Juice of 1 lime (about 3 tablespoons)

PREPARATION
In a saucepan, mix first the 7 ingredients together, coating the crab claws thoroughly in the flavourings. Cover, place on a fairly high heat and leave for 3–4 minutes, shaking occasionally. While the crab is cooking, make the dip: in a mortar, slightly break up the chillies and garlic. Add the salt and lime juice and mix well. Remove the crab claws from the heat and serve with the prepared dip.

TOM YAM GAI
CHICKEN AND LEMON GRASS SOUP

INGREDIENTS
- 1 boneless chicken breast
- 450ml (¾ pint) water
- 5 small red shallots
- 2 garlic cloves
- 1 large dried red chilli
- 1 teaspoon salt
- 1 stalk of lemon grass, cut into 5cm (2in) lengths and slightly crushed
- 4 kaffir lime leaves
- 1 tablespoon fish sauce
- 1 teaspoon sugar
- 1 tablespoon lemon juice
- Coriander to garnish

This is a northern dish. The word yam on its own means spicy, but is usually reserved for spicy salads; when joined with tom, which means liquid, however, the two together equal spicy soup. Given the unusual combination of lemony flavours with the sharpness of chilli and shallot balanced by the simplicity of the chicken, this long yet manageable recipe is well worth the effort.

PREPARATION
In advance, prepare the stock by boiling the chicken breast in the water until it is cooked through, about 10 minutes. Remove the chicken and allow it to cool, then tear the meat into small shreds and set aside.

Next, cover the shallots, garlic and chilli with an envelope of kitchen foil and place under a preheated grill, turning once, until you smell rich charred aroma. Remove, place the contents of the foil parcel in a mortar with the salt and pound to a paste. Set aside. In a large pan, reheat the stock, stir in the paste and simmer. Add the shredded chicken and crushed lemon grass, and return to the boil. Add the lime leaves, fish sauce and sugar. Stir briefly, then remove from the heat – do not overcook. Off the heat, stir in the lemon juice (this must not be boiled with the other ingredients as heated lemon juice completely alters the flavour). As soon as the lemon juice has been added, pour the soup into a tureen, garnish with coriander and serve.

TAO HOU TOD
FRIED FRESH BEANCURD WITH SWEET NUT SAUCE

INGREDIENTS
- Fresh beancurd, see right
- Oil for deep-frying
- 5 tablespoons rice vinegar
- 4 tablespoons sugar
- 1 teaspoon salt
- 3 small fresh red chillies, finely chopped
- 2 tablespoons ground roast peanuts
- Coriander leaves to garnish

Different Oriental and health-food stores sell different shapes and sizes of fresh beancurd, so adapt whatever you can find to get something similar to this. Basically you need 4 blocks of beancurd measuring about 6cm (2½in) square and about 2.5cm (1in) deep. You may obtain such blocks easily as it is a fairly common size, if not, you will have to cut them from a larger block. Whatever the size; the beancurd will probably be sold in a plastic container, with a little soya milk to keep it moist. Remove the block from the container and place it on something like a baking tray to drain. Next take the 4 blocks and cut them diagonally from corner to corner to make 16 triangular shapes.

PREPARATION
Ensure that the beancurd triangles are as dry as possible. Heat the oil for deep-frying, gently ease in the triangles and fry until golden brown. Remove and place on kitchen paper to drain.

In a saucepan, heat the vinegar, sugar and salt until the mixture thickens. Remove from the heat, add the chillies and ground peanuts and stir until thoroughly mixed. Turn into a serving bowl, garnish with coriander leaves and serve with the deep-fried fresh beancurd.

JIN PING
GRILLED MARINATED PORK

INGREDIENTS
- 2 tablespoons finely chopped garlic
- 1 tablespoon finely chopped coriander root
- 1 teaspoon salt
- 1 teaspoon dark soy sauce
- 1 tablespoon light soy sauce
- 500g (6oz) (1¼lb) lean pork fillet, sliced into thin strips 5cm (2in) long
- Satay sticks

FOR THE CHILLI DIP:
- 2 tablespoons fish sauce
- ½ teaspoon dried red chillies, finely chopped
- 1 teaspoon sugar
- 1 tablespoon lime juice

Jin is a northern word for the southern Thai moo – pig or pork – and this dish is a sort of northern satay with a hot sauce. I have suggested the classic Thai chilli dip, but a whole range of hot sauces and dips throughout this book could be used instead.

PREPARATION
In a large bowl, mix the first 5 ingredients. Add the pork and turn them to coat them well in the mixture. Leave to marinate for 1 hour.

Preheat the grill to moderate. Skewer 2 strips of pork on each satay stick, line them up under the grill and cook until seared on each side.

Meanwhile, make the chilli dip by mixing all the ingredients well. Serve the pork with sticky rice, the chilli dip in a dipping bowl.

GRATONG MEE KROB
CRISPY NOODLE BASKETS

INGREDIENTS

**FOR THE GRATONG TONG
(GOLDEN FLOWERS) BATTER CASES:**
- 225g (8oz) flour
- ½ teaspoon salt
- 1 egg
- 225ml (8fl oz) water
- Oil for deep-frying

**FOR THE MEE KROB
(CRISPY NOODLES) FILLING:**
- Oil for deep-frying
- 115g (4oz) dried rice vermicelli noodles (see page 11), soaked for 20 minutes then drained
- 2 tablespoons oil
- 1 egg, lightly beaten with 1 tablespoon cold water
- 30g (1oz) beansprouts, very finely chopped
- 1 spring onion, thinly sliced into tiny rings
- 1 medium fresh red chilli, deseeded and slivered lengthways, then chopped into tiny pieces
- 1 whole head of pickled garlic (see page 15), thinly sliced across the bulb to make flower-shaped sections, then halved

FOR THE SAUCE:
- 2 tablespoons oil
- 115g (4oz) ready-fried beancurd, cut into thin slices, then cut again into very small strips, then finally diced into tiny cubes
- 2 garlic cloves, very finely chopped
- 2 small shallots, very finely chopped
- 1 tablespoon light soy sauce
- ½ teaspoon salt
- 4 tablespoons sugar
- 4 teaspoons vegetable stock (see page 14)
- 3 tablespoons lemon juice
- ½ teaspoon chilli powder

Gratong tong ('golden baskets', or 'golden flowers') are little batter cases with a savoury stuffing, usually served as appetizers or as party snacks. Mee krob are sweet crispy noodles served to counterbalance the strong savoury flavours of a curry or similar dish. Here, I have brought the two together, and the result could be served on its own as finger-food or, again, used as an accompaniment to curry. This is a long and complex recipe, but the results are very rewarding and impressive. There is a special implement for making the baskets, but you could use a small ladle with a 5cm (2in) diameter bowl.

PREPARATION

First make the batter cases: in a large bowl, mix the flour and salt. Break in the egg and mix well. Gradually add the water, stirring constantly until you have a thick batter. Leave for 1 hour.

Heat the oil for deep-frying, dip the mould or ladle bowl into the oil, remove and shake off as much oil as you can. Then dip the bowl or ladle into the batter to coat the outer surface and return it to the hot oil. After 20 seconds the case should shake free. Cook until golden brown. Remove, drain on kitchen paper and set aside. Repeat the procedure until all the batter has been used. Prepare the noodles for the filling: heat the oil for deep-frying and deep-fry the noodles until golden brown and crispy. Remove, drain on kitchen paper and set aside. Make the sauce: heat the oil in a wok or deep frying pan and fry the diced beancurd until crisp. Remove, drain and set aside. Add the garlic to the hot oil and fry until golden brown. Remove, drain and set aside.

Fry the shallots until brown, add the soy sauce, salt, sugar, stock and lemon juice and stir well until the mixture begins to caramelize. Add the chilli powder, the reserved beancurd and garlic, and stir until they absorb some of the liquid. Remove from the heat and set aside.

Finish preparing the filling: in another pan, heat the 2 tablespoons oil and drip in the egg mixture to make little dots of fried egg. Remove, drain and set aside. Return the sauce to the heat, crumble in the crispy noodles, breaking them into tiny whiskers and briefly mix. Turn into a large bowl. Add the beansprouts, spring onion, fried egg dots, chilli and pickled garlic. Mix well. With a teaspoon, place a portion of the mee krob filling into each batter case, arrange on a platter, then serve.

YAM KRABI
KRABI SEAFOOD SALAD

INGREDIENTS
- 2 garlic cloves, very finely chopped
- 4 small fresh red or green chillies, very finely chopped
- 2 tablespoons roasted peanuts, crushed
- 1 tablespoon sugar
- 3 tablespoons fish sauce
- 3 tablespoons lime juice
- Lettuce leaves
- 1 small onion, thinly sliced and separated into rings
- 115g (4oz) pineapple segments
- 60g (2oz) baby squid, chopped into small rings
- 60g (2oz) raw prawns, peeled, deveined and halved lengthways
- 60g (2oz) shelled mussels
- 60g (2oz) shelled baby clams
- 60g (2oz) fish balls (see page 19), halved
- Coriander to garnish

There are dozens of variants of yam, the Thai hot-and-sour salads that are often brought out just before the meal proper, to be eaten with drinks like whisky or other spirits. This version is a speciality of the Krabi Resort and is perfect when eaten by the sea, while listening to the waves and watching the fishing boats leave harbour. Ultra-fresh ingredients are essential, as the recipe is very simple and relies entirely on natural flavours enhanced by a small amount of added spiciness.

PREPARATION

In a bowl, mix the garlic, chilli, peanuts, sugar, fish sauce and lime juice to make a dressing. Set aside.

Place the lettuce leaves, onion rings and pineapple segments in a large bowl and set aside.

Place all the seafood and fish ball halves into a pan, add the reserved dressing and heat, stirring rapidly for the brief time it takes to just cook the ingredients, probably no more than a minute. Turn this out on the salad, toss well, garnish with coriander and serve.

MIAN PLA
FISH, GINGER AND LIME SALAD

INGREDIENTS
- Oil for deep-frying
- 1 whole mackerel or similar oily fish (tuna, etc.)
- 1 tablespoon very finely diced ginger
- 1 tablespoon very finely chopped lime rind
- 10 small red shallots, thinly sliced
- 4–5 small fresh red or green chillies, thinly sliced
- 1 tablespoon lime juice
- ½ teaspoon salt
- 1 teaspoon sugar
- 2 tablespoons roasted peanuts
- 2 spring onions, finely chopped
- Small firm lettuce leaves (Cos, Iceberg, hearts etc.)

As you can guess from the title, this dish has some pretty sparky flavours, very good for a hot summer's lunch or, better still, a picnic. You could also use it as a stand-by recipe, using large tinned sardines for the fish.

PREPARATION

Heat the oil for deep-frying, then deep-fry the fish until golden brown. Remove and drain on kitchen paper. When cool, use your fingers to break the fish into small pieces, removing any bones.

Place the pieces of fish in a large bowl and add all the other ingredients, except the lettuce leaves. Stir well and serve with the lettuce leaves, which are used as scoops to gather up the mixture.

GAENG KIOW WAN NUA
BEEF IN GREEN CURRY WITH COCONUT

INGREDIENTS

- 125ml (4fl oz) coconut cream
- 2 tablespoons oil
- 1 garlic clove, finely chopped
- 2 tablespoons fish sauce
- 1 teaspoon sugar
- 175g (6oz) diced lean beef
- 125ml (4fl oz) beef stock (see page 14) or water
- 2 kiffir lime leaves, chopped
- 3 small green aubergines, quartered
- 15 holy basil leaves

FOR THE GREEN CURRY PASTE:

- 2 long fresh green chillies, roughly chopped
- 10 small fresh green chillies, roughly chopped
- 1 tablespoon chopped lemon grass
- 3 small shallots, roughly chopped
- 4 garlic cloves, roughly chopped
- 2.5cm (1in) galangal, peeled and chopped
- 3 coriander roots, roughly chopped
- 1 teaspoon ground coriander seeds
- ½ teaspoon ground cumin
- ½ teaspoon ground white pepper
- 1 teaspoon finely chopped kaffir lime rind
- 2 teaspoons shrimp paste (see page 14)
- 1 teaspoon salt

Thai curries are more like soups or stews than the thicker Indian varieties, and date from a time before the dry trade spices of the sub-continent became widely available. Although dried spices are now used in curry paste, the final dish depends as much on herb or seed flavours, making the final mix very refreshing and light.

PREPARATION

First make the green curry paste: in a mortar, pound each of the ingredients together in turn to form a thick paste. This will produce about 3 tablespoons of paste; you will need only 1 tablespoon for this recipe, and the rest can be kept in a sealed jar in the refrigerator for up to three weeks and used in other dishes.

In a saucepan, gently heat the coconut cream, but do not allow it to boil. Set aside. In a wok, heat the oil and fry the garlic until it is golden brown. Add 1 tablespoon of the green curry paste and break it up in the oil. Then pour in the warmed coconut cream and stir until the liquid thickens. Add the fish sauce and sugar and stir, then add the beef and cook until it turns brown. Add the stock or water and continue cooking for 3-4 minutes, stirring from time to time. When the beef is just cooked through, stir in the lime leaves. Then stir in the aubergines and basil leaves. Cook for another minute, then serve.

PENANG GAI
PENANG DRY CHICKEN CURRY

INGREDIENTS

- 2 tablespoons oil
- 2 garlic cloves, finely chopped
- 1 tablespoon Red Curry Paste (see page 43)
- 225g (8oz) boneless chicken breast, thinly sliced
- 125ml (4fl oz) coconut cream
- 1 tablespoon ground roasted peanuts
- 20 fresh sweet basil leaves
- 1 long fresh red chilli, finely slivered lengthways
- 2 kaffir lime leaves, rolled into a cigarette shape and thinly sliced across

This recipe is named for the island of Penang, off Malaysia's western coast.

PREPARATION

Heat the oil in a wok or deep frying pan and fry the garlic until it is golden brown. Add the curry paste and stir well.

Add all the remaining ingredients in turn, except the chilli and lime leaves, stirring well between each addition. Stir-fry until the chicken is just cooked through. Turn out on to a serving dish and garnish with the slivers of chilli and kaffir lime leaves.

PAT PET MOO
STIR-FRIED PORK WITH CURRY PASTE

INGREDIENTS

- 225g (8oz) pork and pork skin (see right)
- 2 tablespoons oil
- 2 tablespoons Red Curry Paste (see page 43)
- 6 round aubergines, quartered
- 30g (1oz) krachai (see page 17), very thinly sliced
- 30g (1oz) fresh black peppercorns
- 2 long fresh red chillies, sliced diagonally into thin ovals
- 4 kaffir lime leaves
- 2 tablespoons fish sauce
- 2 tablespoons water
- 1 teaspoon palm sugar (see page 19)
- 20 holy basil leaves

Frugal Thai cooks waste nothing, but if the idea of eating pork skin – other than as crackling – does not appeal, just leave it out and add a little more lean pork. You will need to buy pork chops, cut the meat from the bones (which are discarded or used for stock), cut off the skin and the fat, then cut away the fat from the skin and discard the fat. Cut the pork and the skin into thin slices: it is this that should weigh the required 225g (8oz).

PREPARATION

Heat the oil and stir in the curry paste so that it is well broken up. Add the pork and pork skin, and stir-fry until just cooked through.

Add all the remaining ingredients except the holy basil in turn, stirring between each addition.

Remove from the heat, add the holy basil leaves, stir briefly and serve.

KOW TOM HET
RICE SOUP WITH MUSHROOMS

INGREDIENTS

- 1 tablespoon oil
- 1 garlic clove, finely chopped
- 1.2 litres (2 pints) vegetable stock (see page 14)
- 1 teaspoon preserved vegetable (see page 15)
- 275g (10oz) boiled rice
- ½ teaspoon salt
- 60g (2oz) shiitake mushrooms (dried Chinese mushrooms), soaked for 20 minutes, squeezed dry, the stalks removed, then roughly sliced
- 60g (2oz) dried black fungus mushrooms, soaked, dried and sliced
- 60g (2oz) small whole champignons de Paris
- 30g (1oz) celery, finely chopped
- 30g (1oz) carrot, very finely diced
- 2 spring onions, finely chopped
- A sprinkling of ground black pepper
- Garlic oil to serve

PREPARATION

In a wok, heat the oil and fry the garlic until golden brown. Remove from the heat and reserve both oil and garlic together.

In a saucepan, heat the stock and add the preserved vegetable, cooked rice and salt. Bring to the boil, stir and simmer for a few minutes, until the rice swells and softens. Add the mushrooms, stir well and add all the remaining ingredients. Cook for 2 minutes.

Pour into bowls and dribble a little garlic oil over each before serving.

GAENG LUANG PLA
YELLOW CURRY WITH FISH

INGREDIENTS
- 1.2 litres (2 pints) water
- 175g (6oz) bamboo shoots
- 225g (8oz) fillets of fish (any kind of strong-fleshed fish, such as monkfish, that can stand up to being boiled without falling apart)
- 2 tablespoons tamarind water (see page 19)
- 2 tablespoons fish sauce
- 1 teaspoon sugar

FOR THE CURRY PASTE:
- 2 tablespoons roughly chopped lemon grass
- 1 tablespoon chopped kaffir lime rind
- 10 small shallots
- 12 garlic cloves
- 1 tablespoon roughly chopped fresh turmeric
- 1 teaspoon shrimp paste (see page 14)
- ½ teaspoon salt
- 10 small dried red chillies, soaked for 15 minutes then drained

Yellow curry is a southern speciality, thought to be particularly suited to fish and seafood as it goes well with the saltiness of such maritime ingredients.

PREPARATION
First make the curry paste: in a mortar, pound the lemon grass until well broken up, then add each of the remaining ingredients in turn, pounding well until worked into a paste. Set aside.

In a pan, heat half the water and, as it comes to the boil, stir in 2 tablespoons of the prepared curry paste (the rest can be kept in a sealed jar in the refrigerator for up to 3 weeks and used in other dishes). Add the bamboo shoots and stir well, then add the fish but do not stir. Add the remaining water and gently bring to the boil, simmer and add the tamarind water, fish sauce and sugar. Bring back to the boil, then serve.

PAD PRIK KING NUA PAD BUNG
FRIED BEEF WITH MORNING GLORY

INGREDIENTS
- 2 tablespoons oil
- 225g (8oz) beef steak, thinly sliced
- 175g (6oz) morning glory (water spinach, see page 17), cut into 5cm (2in) lengths
- 2 tablespoons fish sauce
- 1 teaspoon sugar
- 4 kaffir lime leaves, finely chopped

FOR THE RED CURRY PASTE:
- 2 tablespoons roughly chopped lemon grass
- 1½ tablespoons roughly chopped galangal
- 1 tablespoon roughly chopped kaffir lime rind
- 5 small dried red chillies, soaked for 15 minutes then drained and roughly chopped
- 2 large dry red chillies, soaked for 15 minutes then drained and roughly chopped
- 4 garlic cloves
- 6 small red shallots
- ¼ teaspoon salt

PREPARATION
First make the red curry paste: in a mortar, pound together each of the ingredients in turn to form a paste. Drain the chillies and chop them roughly.

In a wok, heat the oil and stir in the curry paste. When well mixed, add the meat and stir until just cooked through.

Add the morning glory and stir well. Add the fish sauce, sugar and kaffir lime leaves, stir well until the morning glory stems have slightly softened, then turn out on a dish and serve.

PLA NUNG MANAO

STEAMED FISH WITH LIME

INGREDIENTS

- 1 whole fish (trout, bream, carp, mullet or salmon will do), about 675g (1½lb), cleaned
- 1 whole lime, thinly sliced into very thin rounds

FOR THE SAUCE:

- 2 garlic cloves, finely chopped
- 2 stalks of coriander with roots, finely chopped
- 4–5 small fresh red or green chillies, finely chopped
- 2 tablespoons fish sauce
- 2 tablespoon lime juice
- 1 teaspoon finely chopped lime rind
- 1 teaspoon sugar

PREPARATION

Place the fish on a plate and cover with lime rounds. Bring some water to the boil in the bottom compartment of a steamer. When boiling, place the fish on its plate in the upper compartment and steam for 15–20 minutes, depending on the variety (e.g. trout needs less time than salmon), until just cooked through.

In the meantime, mix all the sauce ingredients in a bowl.

When the fish has steamed, remove and transfer to a serving dish. Pour over the sauce and serve.

TOD MAN GUNG

DEEP-FRIED PRAWN AND SWEETCORN CAKES

INGREDIENTS

- 20 black peppercorns
- 2 garlic cloves
- ¼ teaspoon salt
- 4 small dried red chillies
- Fresh sweetcorn kernels, scraped from 3 uncooked cobs
- 225g (8oz) chopped raw prawns
- 1 tablespoon fish sauce
- 1 teaspoon sugar
- Oil for deep-frying

FOR THE FRESH PICKLE:

- 4 tablespoons rice vinegar
- 2 teaspoons sugar
- ½ teaspoon salt
- 30g (1oz) cucumber, finely diced
- 1 small carrot, finely diced
- 1 small fresh red or green chilli, finely chopped

PREPARATION

In a mortar, pound together the peppercorns, garlic, salt and dried chillies to form a paste. Add the sweetcorn and pound well into the paste. Add the raw prawns, fish sauce and sugar and pound well.

You should now have a thick paste, which you mould into about 10 round patties about 5cm (2in) in diameter. Deep-fry the patties in batches in the oil until golden, then drain.

While the patties are frying, make the fresh pickle: in a bowl, thoroughly mix all the ingredients.

Serve the cooked patties with the fresh pickle in a small side dish.

KOW NIEW TAT

SWEET STICKY RICE CAKES

INGREDIENTS

- 85g (3oz) uncooked black beans (see page 19)
- 225g (8oz) uncooked sticky rice
- 450ml (1 pint) coconut milk
- 85g (3oz) sugar
- 2 teaspoons salt
- 225ml (8fl oz) coconut cream

PREPARATION

Soak the black beans in water for at least 6 hours. About 3 hours before you plan to begin, soak the sticky rice in water.

While the rice is soaking, drain the black beans. Place them in a pan with fresh water and bring to the boil. The water will turn black. Remove from the heat and pour away the water. Repeat this whole process twice. Bring to the boil for the last time. Check that the beans have softened; when they have, drain and set aside.

Place the coconut milk in a bowl with half the sugar and half the salt and mix well. Set aside. Drain the rice and turn into a small baking tray, spreading evenly. Pour over the coconut milk, sugar and salt mixture, place the tray in the upper compartment of a steamer and steam for 20 minutes. Meantime, mix the coconut cream with the remaining sugar and salt in a bowl. When the rice has nearly cooked, open the steamer and pour over this coconut cream mixture. Cover and steam for a further 5 minutes, then lift the cover and sprinkle the black beans over the surface. Cover and steam for a final 5 minutes. Remove the tray and allow to cool, cut the cake into blocks 2.5cm (1in) square and serve.

PAD THAI

THAI FRIED NOODLES

INGREDIENTS

- 4 tablespoons oil
- 2 garlic cloves, finely chopped
- 1 egg
- 175g (6oz) medium flat rice flour noodles, soaked for 20 minutes then drained
- 2 tablespoons lemon juice
- 1½ tablespoons fish sauce
- ½ teaspoon sugar
- 2 tablespoons dried shrimp, or 5 fresh prawns, or 115g (4oz) chicken, pork or beef, thinly sliced
- 2 tablespoons chopped roasted peanuts
- ½ teaspoon chilli powder
- 1 tablespoon preserved white radish (see page 19), finely chopped
- 30g (1oz) beansprouts
- 2 spring onions, cut into 2.5cm/2in pieces
- Coriander and lemon wedges to garnish

This is so much the classic Thai fast food dish that I have felt obliged to include a version of it here.

PREPARATION

Heat the oil in a wok or deep frying pan, and fry the garlic until golden brown. Break the egg into the pan and stir rapidly to scramble with the garlic. Add the noodles and stir well, scraping all the ingredients together.

One by one, add the following ingredients, stirring once between each addition: lemon juice, fish sauce, sugar, the main ingredient of choice, half the peanuts, half the chilli powder, the preserved radish, half the beansprouts, and the spring onions. Stir constantly. Test the noodles for tenderness and check that the main ingredient is just cooked through, then turn out on a warmed serving plate. Arrange the remaining peanuts, beansprouts and chilli powder on the side so that the diner can mix them in at will. Garnish with coriander and lemon wedges, and serve.

NAM PRIK GUNG POW
GRILLED PRAWN SPICY DIP

INGREDIENTS
- 115g (4oz) fresh prawns in the shell
- 10 small fresh red chillies
- 10 small red shallots
- 6 garlic cloves
- 1 teaspoon shrimp paste (see page 14)
- 1 tablespoon lime juice
- 2 tablespoons fish sauce
- 2 teaspoons sugar

Like all nam prik spicy dips, this should be served with a choice of raw vegetables, such as morning glory (water spinach) and pea aubergines, or fresh crisp salad vegetables, such as lettuce and cucumber. You can also serve it with small deep-fried fish, like sardines.

PREPARATION

Grill the prawns until just cooked through, then peel and devein them and roughly chop. Set aside.

In a mortar, pound together the chillies, shallots, garlic and shrimp paste to form a paste, then add the reserved prawn pieces and lightly pound (not to a paste).

Add the lime juice, fish sauce and sugar and stir well. Serve with a choice of accompaniments as suggested above.

KAI WAN
SWEET GINGER EGGS

INGREDIENTS
- 450ml (¾ pint) water
- 4 tablespoons sugar
- 1 tablespoon ginger, slivered into fine matchsticks
- 2 eggs

Eating an egg as a dessert, other than mixed into pastry or custard, will probably be an acquired taste for most in the West, though it was a practice introduced to Thailand by the Portuguese. However, this recipe is so simple and the ingredients so easy to obtain, it has to be worth the risk!

PREPARATION

In a saucepan, bring the water, sugar and ginger to the boil. Lower the heat and simmer until the liquid reduces to a light syrup. Return to the boil. Crack open the eggs and let the contents drip into the syrup with a circular movement of the hand, so that strands of cooked egg form in the hot liquid. The egg cooks almost immediately, so when both eggs are dripped into the syrup, quickly remove the pan from the heat. Spoon the syrup and egg into dessert bowls and serve.

Laos

BUDDHA, LITTLE RICHARD AND BUFFALO MINCE

A monk adjusts his robe

I expected many things from my first visit to Laos in 1994 – mainly the usual images of a forgotten Shangri-La, of cloud-topped mountains and faraway villages lost in the mist. What I hadn't expected was to end up in a brand-new discotheque on the night this isolated, landlocked nation took another lurch away from its communist past.

The friend who picked me up at the airport had arranged lunch at a pretty terraced restaurant in one of Vientiane's surviving colonial villas. The meal was classic French bistro fare – pâté followed by a grill with chips and salad – and during it I got into conversation with the owner, a resilient Frenchman with a mysterious past that sounded like something out of a Somerset Maugham story. By his own account he had had a run-in with the criminal underworld in Bangkok before he made his way to safety in Laos. Now he was about to open the country's first real disco with non-stop recorded music. My friend explained that this was illegal as the government insists that live groups perform at least part of the time. Not only that, the new club would stay open long into the night, thus infringing an 11.30 curfew that was still in force. Intrigued, we decided to take the risk and accept his invitation to join him later that evening for the grand opening.

While I was a little surprised to be eating my first meal in Laos in a French bistro, I soon learned that this was almost inevitable – most restaurants exist for the expatriate community, business people and aid workers. Indeed, modern Vientiane is very much a French colonial creation, the remotest of France's Indo-Chinese capitals, a mere shadow of mighty Hanoi, the real seat of power. Vientiane is too new to be a major Laotian cultural centre and its main charm lies in the remaining vestiges of its former Frenchness – the occasional Anglo-Norman villa, people carrying baguettes home from small bakeries, and the French and Italian restaurants near the fountain at the centre of the town's tiny commercial district, where members of the small foreign community gather for their evening apéritif.

Until recently, the suppression of private enterprise by the communists meant that few Laotian eating places survived. In any case, hospitality has traditionally been very much home-based. When you pass someone's house in Laos, the occupants don't ask how you are, they say: 'Have you eaten?' It is the country's basic greeting and if you haven't, then you will certainly be invited to do so. Indeed you can always recognize one of the few Laotian restau-rants by the presence of a water jar and drinking ladle near the entrance, a gift for any passing traveller who needs refreshment.

I saw some of these in the area round the main market, which I visited after that first lunch. The market buildings were dreary concrete sheds in the neo-Brutalist manner beloved of oppressive regimes, but the stalls inside offered all the usual colours and scents of Asia. At first glance this seemed little different from the great food emporia of Bangkok or Chiang Mai – piles of mangoes, mounds of small green aubergines. As I was to discover throughout my extended tour of Southeast Asia, the one thing that unites the region is the similarity of its markets. Every major town in every country has a huge central sales area, a large covered space, usually built by the government. The older ones are often beautiful wooden palaces made of soaring spars and arches, like the inside of an upturned boat. Newer models, like the market in Vientiane, are rather dull concrete shells.

However, nothing can repress the sheer exuberance of the sights and smells that confront the visitor once inside, for ranged along alleyways will be stall after stall piled high with the bounty of Asia. Particular products tend to be kept together, so you will get a cluster of vegetable sellers, with cleverly constructed arrangements of brightly coloured plants and leaves: pyramids of rich red shallots, sweeping curls of emerald longbeans, twisted fingers of ginger and galangal. Some specialize in one item, so you find stacked baskets of bright red chillies of all sizes, with surprisingly big and bulbous varieties – though it is the little tiny ones that turn out to be the most ferociously hot. Many things come in ready-to-buy bundles – five stems of lemon grass tied with a neat raffia bow, four little silver river fish carefully laid side-by-side in a round woven container. The fruit sellers have the easiest time: their heaps of lopped pineapples or purply-red mangosteens are irresistible. Every market has its meat section, with the butchers ceaselessly at work chopping and cutting – for in lands where refrigeration is still novel, livestock are always killed, sold, cooked and eaten the same day.

Indeed it is the freshness of everything, much helped by the endless splashing of water and the swish of hand fans to keep away the insects, that makes the market so tinglingly alive. There are cascades of cut flowers, orchids in huge bunches, and lots of

Fisherman on the Mekong

small homemade things – sweets and grills, and other prepared dishes brought in by local women who hope to make a little ready cash selling their specialities – some grilled fish balls with a hot-and-sweet sauce, sweetcorn fritters with a fresh pickle of cucumber and tomato in rice vinegar. In Laos you will always find someone offering links of sausages made of pork, herbs and chilli, hung from a bamboo pole. As in northern Thailand, charcuterie is a speciality, with villagers smoking any extra meat over open fires.

All Asian markets are eating places too, with food hawkers parking their hand-pulled cooking wagons in the surrounding streets, some selling noodles briefly dipped in a rich broth, others fried rice with roast duck, or sweets such as sticky rice and fruit steamed in banana leaf or little bowls of iced coconut cream and melon. This is the best restaurant in the world – and probably the cheapest, as the more adventurous visitor quickly discovers. The surroundings may be scruffy, and it is usually better not to look too closely at the ground, but individual cleanliness is always impeccable. As long as there's a nearby source of running water everything will be thoroughly washed, and the fact that most things are cooked at the last minute considerably reduces any risk of infection. Almost all Southeast Asian food is rapidly produced

Village boys washing their cattle

once the rather long process of preparing the ingredients is complete. Even our curries are made then and there, not stewed or reheated.

In fact the name 'curry' tends to confuse those new to our food who know only the modern Indian curry, with its thick rich sauces and its heavy reliance on pounded dry spices. In fact, that sort of curry is a fairly recent development in Indian cuisine. Our curries, lighter and more liquid – and sometimes called soups – are pretty much as they used to be all over Asia, including India, before the spread of the spice trade and the arrival of the chilli from South America. In the original curries, the sharp flavours and the 'heat' were obtained from vegetables, herbs and herb seeds – mustard, fennel, garlic, coriander root, coriander seed, etc. The result was a pungent refreshing liquid that was taken in small quantities to give a lift to other, blander dishes, mainly to help eat greater quantities of rice than would otherwise be possible. The idea of eating a curry as a single dish is not in the order of things – in fact, the only single dishes we eat are lunch-time noodles or fried rice. Otherwise a real meal is a balanced combination of several different dishes, of which a curry could be one (see 'Making a Meal', page 188).

The arrival and spread of the dry or 'trade' spices are crucial parts of the history of Southeast Asian food and, as I was learning

in Laos, it is a tale that is not yet complete. Indeed, this whole book is inevitably open-ended, for our cooking is not a finite, complete thing, but a constantly evolving story, with new elements arriving ever more quickly now that air travel and modern communications can spread products and processes with such astonishing speed – soon every city in the region, including Vientiane, will have its McDonalds and its sushi bar side by side.

However, if you want to get to the heart of what is still the unique taste of our food you have to let your nose lead you to the section of the market where the main pickles and preserves are on sale. This won't be hard because, if you are new to Southeast Asia, these will be the smells – stinks you might call them – that have been bothering you since you arrived. The aroma is fish and not fresh at all, sticky heaps of purple paste, earthenware jars with muddy-looking lumps of something unrecognizable, but certainly not attractive, and bottles of light brown liquid with gaudily coloured labels.

Fish, especially river fish, is the main protein source of Southeast Asian cooking – our rivers teem with fish, they even swim down our city streets during the monsoon floods. There are so many fish, a lot of them too small for immediate eating, that we can transform them into our main flavourings by fermenting them, pressed with salt, in large 'Ali-Baba' earthenware jars. This pickling process, whereby the fish are left to rot, gives two main products: a liquid known as fish sauce that is drained off and filtered then bottled, and fermented fish. Fish sauce is our main savoury flavouring; the best is light brown and has a refreshingly salty taste, the worst is dark and bitter. The fermented fish itself can be used as an ingredient on its own or can be liquidized to give a stronger-tasting flavouring than the lighter fish sauce.

The powerful odour of fermented or pickled fish is the one thing that most offends people from the West, where putrefaction is now associated with things that are dangerous and unhealthy – yet the Europeans of antiquity were perfectly familiar with such things and we know that the ancient Romans flavoured their food with liquamen or garum, which seem to have been almost identical to our fish sauce. The good news is that, once cooked, the fermented fish is transformed into the pleasant savoury taste that is unique to our cuisine. This is then built on by the various high-notes that each country prefers – the lemon/lime flavours of Thailand, the coconut cream sauces of Malaysia and the mint tastes of Vietnam.

For me, the greatest pleasure in visiting a market in a new country is teasing out the little differences that will give a clue to what is unusual about the cooking I am about to enjoy. In Vientiane I discovered a larger variety of galangal than is found elsewhere in Southeast Asia, and an edible river weed – a sort of freshwater seaweed – unique to Laos. What impresses the first-time visitor, however, is the enormous quantity and variety of salad vegetables – lettuces, cucumbers, tomatoes, longbeans, white cabbages, mint and morning glory (water spinach). As I was soon to learn, a salad is served with almost every meal in Laos and certainly at all feasts and parties. These are not like the mild salads common in the

Market scene, Vientiane

West. The Laotian salad, or laap, is a hot spicy dish, sometimes brought out before the main meal and eaten as an appetizer with an apéritif, usually a strong spirit like whisky. The word laap means something like 'luck' – if you win the lottery that is laap, so eating a little of something that might bring you good fortune is clearly a wise move.

This is one of many dishes and words that has crossed the Mekong to Thailand, though we pronounce the word so that it sounds more like laab. In fact, there are more Lao living in Thailand than in Laos, and the Thai province of Issan is basically Lao in everything from dress to food. Lao is, of course, the name of the ethnic group, while a Laotian is a citizen of Laos whatever his or her racial origins. Having settled first in the mountainous North, the Lao, whether in modern-day Laos or northern Thailand, cultivate sticky or glutinous rice, rather than the fluffy fragrant variety grown in the flat paddies of the southern plains and, being so far from the coast where coconut palms abound, Laotian food relies far less on coconut milk and cream. For the same reason, Indian and Arab traders were unable to bring the dry spices, like cumin, star anise, cardamom, cinnamon, etc., which have become key elements in the cooking of the coastal areas. Traditional Lao cuisine still depends more on herb-based flavours – holy and sweet basil, fresh coriander leaf and dill – though the chilli did gradually make its way north during the four centuries since its arrival on the distant seaboard.

There was, however, a difference between the food eaten by ordinary people and that served by the chefs at the Laotian royal court, who were able to import coconuts and dry spices and who maintained a refined, highly flavoured cuisine quite different from the food found at village level. Today, with Laos opening up its borders to trade with Thailand and Vietnam, those once rare ingredients are more readily available in the main towns. One result is that Nam Ngua, a noodle soup with beef and mint leaves, and flavoured with cinnamon and star anise (see page 62), has become one of the most popular fast-food dishes on the stalls of Vientiane and other centres. Out in the villages, however, such 'exotic' ingredients are still virtually unknown.

While visiting the market, I decided to have a quick snack before my evening on the dance floor, and rather unadventurously decided to have what the Laotians call Tam Som. This perfectly illustrates the closeness between Laos and Thailand. We Thais call the dish Som Tam, but it's the same mix of shredded raw papaya with crushed chillies, garlic, nuts, tomato and longbeans, flavoured with fish sauce and tempered with a little sugar – served, of course, with a basket of sticky rice (see page 67). This would seem to indicate that the recipe was originally from the North, even though today it is eaten right across Southeast Asia.

This proximity between the two nations is not just evident in food. Thailand and Laos share a similar language and culture. We practise the same form of Buddhism and our architecture – from gilded temples to simple teak houses – is almost identical. Today, we are growing even closer – a fact made evident when I arrived at the new disco. The place was already hopping when I walked in, and it was obvious that almost everything on show that night, from the music to the style of dance and dress, were all from across the Mekong, gleaned from Thai television, beamed to Laos from the Thai city of Nong Khai on the opposite bank.

It could hardly be otherwise – the two countries are historically and culturally intertwined – at one point the Lao ruled both sides of the river; later the Thai reversed the situation, making Laos a subject state. The only significant differences were brought about by the years of French colonial rule, which kept us apart. This was continued with the policy of isolation imposed by the communists following the near destruction of the country by American planes, ordered to bomb the Laotian side of the Ho Chi Minh Trail during the Vietnam War. More bombs were dropped on Laos than were exploded during the whole of the Second World War and even today there are large parts of the country that are still scattered with unexploded shells.

The war and the years of repression after the Pathet Lao established their hold on the country in the mid-seventies drove most of the business community into exile in Thailand. Many became highly successful entrepreneurs and are now hoping to return, bringing with them the skills needed to relaunch a moribund economy. You get a real sense of the differences between Thailand and Laos on the banks of the Mekong, where I went for a stroll after my session at the club. It was obvious that no one was bothering about the curfew, though there were not many people about. Vientiane stretches along the Mekong in a thin line, from the airport in the north to the southern landing-stage about 22km from the city centre. From here ferries cross to Nong Khai, whose glaring lights burn through the night, neon signs advertising its clubs and late-night restaurants. On the Laotian bank there were just a few noodle stalls, lit by dangling low-wattage electric bulbs. This used to be a tree-lined promenade of pleasant colonial villas, though today many have been replaced by seedy-looking Soviet-style blocks.

**The morning drum,
Luang Prabang**

Statues in the Wat Si
Muang Temple, Vientiane

I picked my noodle stall and chose the spicy nam ngua, pleased with its rich spread of flavours, from the beef stock to the pungent star anise, balanced by the plain white noodles. It was a perfect evening – with so little artificial light I could see the stars quite clearly. Indeed 30 years of near-complete isolation have meant that Laos has been virtually untouched by the capitalist explosion that has transformed so much of Asia. The drive from Vientiane's Watay Airport into the town was a vintage car enthusiast's dream: fifties' Mercedes with Cadillac wings, early model Volkswagens that were clearly built to last, Peugeots out of old French films. Relics of the recent past were everywhere – in the lobby of the Asian Pavilion Hotel there was an Intourist poster of a Russian onion-domed church, while the shop on the opposite corner offered hand-tinted postcards of a Laotian girl in Chinese-style military jacket and red-star cap, manipulating the dials of an antiquated transmitter, with the English caption 'An Operator Lao', in case you hadn't guessed.

Of course all this is changing fast. The year before my visit, General Kaysone Phomivane finally died. He had been one of the last of the old-guard hard-line dictators and while his successors are barely any younger, they at least know that time is up and have

begun to ease open the prison door. In fact their real problem is not letting in the world, but holding it at arm's length, so that the country is not thrown into chaos by hordes of returning exiles eager to rush headlong towards capitalism no matter what effect this has on a people still living a quiet traditional life – which, for all its drawbacks in terms of poverty, still offers much that is gentle and worthwhile.

To see this way of life at its best, one has to get away from the present-day capital, travelling north into the mountains to the point where the Mekong meets the Nam Khan river, site of the ancient city of Luang Prabang. Once capital of the whole country, then the chief city of a semi-autonomous province and always the nation's spiritual centre, Luang Prabang is tiny and resolutely unmodern – a mix of temples and crumbling colonial houses, with the occasional Chinese mansion dotted among tree-shaded paths that criss-cross the promontory where the two rivers touch. Unlike Vientiane, with its glass and concrete office blocks, this is Southeast Asia as it used to be – a mix of traditional wooden buildings and colonial stucco residences. The town's superb location means that the stroller is constantly offered glimpses of water in the deep valleys on two sides of the triangular settlement, with pleasing views across to the opposite banks, then on to the high mountains beyond.

And there are other surprises. My first full day in the town began before dawn when I was woken by the sound of drumming – deep, sonorous, loud and frightening. It was as if I'd slipped into a dream of ancient warfare, the drumbeats urging the soldiers into battle. Or was it an alarm of some sort? Perhaps the hotel was on fire? I went to see what the nightmare might be and found what appeared to be the entire population out on the streets, some kneeling down, others moving away towards some distant goal. Then I saw what must surely be one of the most amazing sights in Asia: hundreds of saffron-robed monks slowly wending their way along the main streets of the town, each with his alms bowl ready for the morning food collection. In all Buddhist countries you can see little groups of monks and novices collecting their daily meal, but this was on a more spectacular scale.

Luang Prabang is truly a holy place – once there were 66 temples and even today an astonishing 32 still survive, each with a full complement of monks, hence the long winding march. I saw the drum on a high wooden platform nearby. It is sounded before dawn each morning to wake the monks and alert the people to prepare their offerings. As the procession drew closer I began to see an even more extraordinary sight: the kneeling donors were throwing little balls into each passing bowl – very rapidly – one, then another, and another – a ball for each passing figure. Closer up I saw that these were balls of sticky rice, plucked from a basket, hastily rolled, then thrown up into the air and into a bowl. No one ever missed, no doubt as a result of the practice everyone gets.

I now guessed where the others were walking to – they must be going to the food market to buy meals to donate. I followed and quickly came to the large wooden hall where people were buying small plastic bags, tied with rubber bands, containing curries and stir-fried dishes and the inevitable laap – whatever the stalls were offering that day. In the past every household would have prepared something special, but even in that holy place the modern world has made life too rushed for such niceties, so the gifts must be bought. As the procession passed, everyone went out, knelt down and placed the little bags in amongst the balls of sticky rice. Among the watchers was a scattering of hill-tribe peoples, the same minority ethnic groups that live all over the Golden Triangle, in the North of Thailand and Burma as well as in Laos. They are instantly recognizable by their red-and-black woven costumes, the women shackled in silver bangles and necklaces, with silver decorations in their woven hats, the older ones puffing on fat hand-rolled cigarettes bigger than cigars, the children in leggings and pom-pom hats - a sight out of history.

That morning I found a guide called Somphong Sakdi, whose name means 'ping pong', which was appropriate as he was bright and quick and organized everything I asked him to. I wanted to get out of town to see something of village life, so he suggested a boat ride to the Pak Ou caves, two limestone caverns piled high with Buddha images offered by the faithful. Although this was a regular tourist outing, it was still worth seeing the magical grotto, lit first by the glow from the cave entrance then, further in, by the flicker of Somphong's torch.

The journey itself was even more fascinating as it allowed me to see just how much of Laotian life and food depends on the great river. While 70 per cent of the country's land surface consists of the high mountains, broken by plains and forests, that run north to the border with China, the population there is sparse and divided between different ethnic groups, most of whom practise simple 'slash and burn' agriculture. Over half the population is concentrated along the Mekong and its tributaries, and it is their culture that is considered most typically Lao. Their lives are strictly ordered by the Mekong – a rushing torrent during the rainy season, slowing dramatically to a meandering flow during the dry part of the year.

As I was there after the rains, the water was low, leaving the sloping banks exposed and covered in rich silt. By then the gluti-nous rice had already been planted and plots of vegetables were already giving off green shoots. Traditionally a single rice harvest was expected, but where it is possible to irrigate banked-off plots above the high-water mark as many as three crops can be achieved. There will have to be some rotation with other plants, perhaps ground nuts, so as not to exhaust the soil. From the air, the plains of Laos are covered in squared-off plots that, in the rainy season, look like a mosaic of mirror-glass.

Just before planting, the land is turned with buffalo ploughs. Next comes planting, then transplanting the young shoots so that they are not too crowded. After this there is a respite while nature does its work. With time to spare before harvesting, groups of women were panning for minuscule nuggets of gold in the shallows, while the men were huddled round temporary bamboo shelters, where they were boiling up the brew that they distil into a rice liquor that we call Mekong Whiskey. The area along this part of the river was at one time famous for making the huge bulbous earthenware jars used to store the drink, though now the demand for the whiskey is so great that many have to be brought in from elsewhere.

Climbing up the steep bank, we crested the rise and walked straight into a village of about 20 houses, all quite close together and arranged without any apparent sense of order. Built of teak, the houses in this area were not quite high enough to be the tall stilt-houses common in other parts of the region, where the open space beneath the floorboards provides a cool airy dining room or a work space, perhaps with a loom or a coconut-grating machine. Here there was just enough space for storage and a refuge where animals could shelter – I saw pigs, chickens and ducks, all jumbled up with a crowd of tiny children who had hurried to see what this new distraction might be.

Somphong explained that the animals were not for everyday eating but were reserved for feast days. Naturally enough the main ingredient for village meals was the plentiful supply of freshwater fish from the river below. There is a huge variety of river fish in Laos, including the most spectacular of all, the giant pa beuk (the 'elephant fish'), the largest freshwater fish on earth, bigger than a man and enough to feed an entire village – as well as providing a mound of eggs which are as sought after as caviar. Sadly, that legendary giant catfish is now a rarity and the discovery of such a monster a major event.

Happily there's ample ordinary fish in the rivers, both for immediate eating and for pickling in the same large earthenware jars to produce prahok in Laos (pla ra in north-eastern Thailand), which in villages like this one is more than just a flavouring. For most families, on an ordinary day the basic meal is lots of sticky rice with just a very hot spicy dip, a nam prik, made from lumps of pickled fish taken from the jar, and accompanied by some simply blanched vegetables, such as morning glory plucked from near the water's edge.

Apart from pickled fish, the villagers rely on food from the wild. Somphong listed: frogs, snakes, insects, little birds, quail and the small mouse deer as well as a unique species of edible rat. There is also much use of wild herbs for, as my guide made clear, the people of Laos do not differentiate between wild and domesticated food, whether plants or animals, as others tend to do. It is all the same, and freely available, as long as the population remains small and scattered – though as the country opens up and people begin to migrate to the towns this is unlikely to last.

For me, the most wonderful thing about my visit to the village was the sight of water buffalo grazing nearby, a pleasure that has almost disappeared in Thailand, where those lovely beasts have been replaced by the 'mechanical buffalo'. This is an impressive machine that can plough a field, carry crops to market and be used as a generator to power a television set. It has transformed village life, however, making it much more like life in town. Of course, one should not criticize country people for wanting to have an easier and more entertaining existence, but it has also removed some of the sense of community that you still find in Laos.

In the evening all the village children ride the buffaloes down to the river for a drink and a bath – both for animal and child, while the absence of television means that people still rely on each other for friendship and amusement. Much of village life revolves around the temple and its festivities, when huge amounts of food are produced by everyone working together – the men helping to steam the rice, the women stirring great vats of food. The

The low, meandering Mekong during the dry season, near Luang Prabang

The Pha That Luang Temple, Vientiane

Street scene, Vientiane

biggest fête of all comes at the opening of the rainy season, when farming activity ceases and the young men enter the local temple for a brief spell as novice monks, a cause for huge celebration – eating, drinking and dancing.

Even on my brief visit I saw one small scene that said so much about the communal atmosphere that still reigns in that pleasant place. The gang of chattering children led me by the hand to a wooden house full of women – probably all the women in the village – sitting around one of their number who had just given birth to a little girl. I was invited to look in and congratulate her and everyone smiled and muttered their approval, indicating that my presence would prove a lucky omen for the new arrival.

These traces of an earlier, gentler way of life can still be discerned in the nearby city, where the beauty of a former age is visible in the splendour of the red and gold temples, with their shimmering mosaics and gilded Buddhas. For me, however, the most fascinating building was the more recent royal palace, built in 1904 and now a museum. There is an aura of tragedy about this rather plain building, from which the last monarch and his family were led away in 1977, after the communist take-over, for re-education – a euphemism for torture, starvation and death in the northern jungle, near the Vietnamese border. A previous king had had the throne hall redecorated during the swinging sixties and somehow managed to have traditional Laotian murals done in what was then a fashionable pop-art style, with mosaics made of mirror-glass – a curious mix of Buddhism and Sergeant Pepper's Lonely Hearts Club Band.

There has been some attempt to preserve the palace as it was. The private apartments still have their rather ordinary French department-store furniture and are kept as they were on that day when the King and Queen were taken away. But the most important act of preservation was made by a man called Phia Sing, a senior courtier who had been a tutor to the royal princes and later a sort of major domo, responsible for the royal kitchens. In 1974, just before the fall of the monarchy, the then British Ambassador to Laos, Alan Davidson, called on the Crown Prince in Luang Prabang to ask his advice on a book he was writing about fish and seafood. During the course of their conversation Davidson mentioned his difficulty in finding authentic Laotian recipes, whereupon the Prince produced two little notebooks in which the late Phia Sing had kept a record of the dishes produced in the royal kitchens. Fortunately the Prince allowed his visitor to borrow and copy the books, as the take-over by the Pathet Lao, which happened soon after, might well have resulted in their complete loss. In 1980 Davidson was able to arrange for the translation and publication of Phia Sing's notes, thus preserving the entire tradition of Laotian royal cuisine. For my book, I have used mainly village recipes collected during my visit, but I have drawn on some of Phia Sing's royal dishes, adapting them for modern use. Anyone interested in Laotian cuisine will always be grateful for Phia Sing's foresight and Alan Davidson's dedication in ensuring that these precious documents are there for all to use.

When I visited Luang Prabang it was possible to sample something similar to that royal cuisine at the Villa de Princesse Hotel, where the restaurant was run by one of Phia Sing's daughters. Her menu was a blend of Laotian royal dishes with elements of French cooking, a mix that was fashionable in the colonial era, when village cooking was considered crude. Today, of course, it is precisely those simple, homely recipes that we are most concerned to preserve and I asked Somphong if there was anywhere in Luang Prabang where I would find real village fare. He was able to arrange a last lunch in a tiny restaurant on a platform built out from a bank overlooking the Mekong. It was a simple place with no name, furnished with long wooden tables and benches, the only decoration being several rocket-shell cases from what the Laotians call 'the American War', which were now used peacefully as plant pots. There we feasted on river weed flavoured with sesame seeds, minced buffalo meat with eggplant, and a curry steamed in banana leaves, all with an idyllic view across the river to the little

Cultivating sticky rice on the banks of the Mekong

white Champhet Temple, which was peeping out above the distant trees on the far bank.

Back in Vientiane for one last night, I decided to leave the new disco to the town's youth, while I made my way to the old-established night spot in the Hotel Anou. The club dates back to the time when the limit of decadence was a Lao singer doing his own versions of long out-of-date American hits. Today, the Anou is a living museum of pop-culture – at midnight, a wicked half hour after the curfew, I was still happily listening to a tall thin Laotian doing a passable imitation of Little Richard singing 'She's Got It'. Sadly, such a spectacle is unlikely to last, now that the modern world is knocking at the door. While I was there, the first bridge was being built across the Mekong, finally linking Thailand and Laos. This has now opened and a second is planned. Soon Vientiane's lights will rival those of Nong Khai and, with new products flooding in, Laotian cooking may well be transformed out of all recognition. For the moment at least, however, it is still possible to see and to taste a culture and a cuisine that are memories of the past. Laos may not be Shangri-La, but it is certainly the land where time stood still.

NAM NGUA

LAO BEEF NOODLE SOUP WITH MINT LEAVES

INGREDIENTS

- 2 tablespoons vegetable oil
- 2 garlic cloves, finely chopped
- 60g (2oz) beansprouts
- 115g (4oz) fresh rice river noodles, dried, soaked and drained
- 115g (4oz) boneless tender beef, finely slivered
- 20 fresh mint leaves

FOR THE STOCK:

- 450ml (¾ pint) beef stock (see page 14)
- 1 cinnamon stick
- 2 star anise
- 2 tablespoons fish sauce
- 1 tablespoon light soy sauce
- 1 teaspoon sugar
- ½ teaspoon ground white pepper

PREPARATION

Put all the stock ingredients into a large saucepan and bring to the boil, then simmer for 15 minutes.

In the meantime, heat the oil in a small pan and fry the garlic until golden brown. Set aside both the oil and the garlic.

Heat a saucepan of water until it boils. Using a mesh sieve or strainer, plunge the beansprouts into the boiling water. Hold for only a second, remove and drain, then turn into a serving bowl.

Next, plunge in the noodles with the sieve or strainer, leave for 10 seconds then remove and drain. Add to the serving bowl.

As before, plunge in the beef and leave until just cooked through, then remove, drain and place in the bowl.

Finally, add the reserved oil and garlic to the bowl and stir all the ingredients briefly. Scatter over the mint leaves and pour over the hot stock, stir and serve immediately.

KENG KALAMPI

WHITE CABBAGE SOUP

INGREDIENTS

- 1.2 litres (2 pints) pork stock (see page 14)
- 60g (2oz) minced lean pork
- 2 tablespoons fish sauce
- 175g (6oz) white cabbage, coarsely chopped
- 1 egg
- ½ teaspoon sugar
- 5 small shallots (preferably the very red variety), halved
- A grinding of black pepper
- Coriander leaves to garnish

PREPARATION

In a large pan, heat the stock. When it is boiling, drop in small clumps of the minced pork, stirring the liquid to keep the clumps separate while they cook.

Add the fish sauce and stir. Add the cabbage and simmer briefly, then break in the egg and stir rapidly to form ribbons of cooked egg. Add the sugar, the shallot halves and a grinding of black pepper. Simmer until the cabbage leaves soften.

Remove from the heat and ladle into bowls. Garnish with coriander leaves and serve.

KENG BOUAD MAK FAK KHAM
PUMPKIN IN COCONUT SOUP

INGREDIENTS
- 1.2 litres (2 pints) vegetable stock (see page 14)
- 175g (6oz) pumpkin, peeled, cut into thin wedges
- 225ml (8fl oz) coconut milk
- 4 small shallots, grilled until lightly coloured
- 1 teaspoon salt
- ¼ teaspoon ground black pepper
- 3 spring onions, finely chopped

PREPARATION

In a large saucepan, heat the stock. Add the pumpkin and stir well until the liquid is boiling.

Lower the heat to a simmer. Add the coconut milk, shallots, salt and pepper and stir well. Bring back to the boil. The pumpkin should now be cooked.

Stir in the spring onions, turn into a warmed tureen and serve.

PED TOM KHA
DUCK AND GALANGAL SOUP

INGREDIENTS
- 1 tablespoon oil
- 175g (6oz) duck breast, thinly sliced
- 20 thin ovals of galangal (diagonal slices across the 'root', washed only: there is no need to peel galangal)
- 225ml (8fl oz) coconut milk
- 8 small shallots, thinly sliced
- 1.2 litres (2 pints) chicken stock (see page 14)
- 4 tablespoon fish sauce
- 1 teaspoon sugar
- 2 tablespoons lemon juice
- 2 spring onions, finely chopped
- Coriander leaves to garnish

While this is similar to the Thai galangal soup, I was surprised to find duck used in place of chicken. I can't imagine why it has so far been overlooked by Thai cooks, who are usually keen to try anything.

PREPARATION

In a wok or deep frying pan, heat the oil and fry the duck and galangal until they give off a rich aroma.

Stir in the coconut milk and shallots. Stir well, add the stock, fish sauce and sugar, and bring to the boil, continuing to stir.

As soon as it comes to the boil, remove the liquid from the heat and stir in the lemon juice and spring onions.

Pour into bowls, garnish with coriander leaves and serve.

TAM SOM

HOT AND SOUR PAPAYA SALAD

INGREDIENTS

- 2 garlic cloves
- 4 or 5 small fresh red or green chillies
- 2 longbeans, chopped into 5cm (2in) lengths
- 175g (6oz) fine slivers of raw papaya
- 1 tomato, cut into wedges
- 1 tablespoon pickled or fermented fish (see page 14)
- 1 tablespoon fish sauce
- 1 tablespoon sugar
- 2 tablespoons lime juice
- Fresh firm green vegetables, such as longbeans, cabbage, etc.

PREPARATION

In a large mortar, pound the garlic, then add the chillies and pound well again. Add the longbeans, but only break these up slightly. Then, using a spoon to stir well, add the papaya and lightly pound, stirring occasionally. Add the tomato and lightly pound. Stir, then add the pickled or fermented fish, the fish sauce, sugar and lime juice, stirring well. Turn out on a serving dish, with the fresh raw vegetables. Any leaves, such as white cabbage, can be used as a scoop for the spicy mixture.

LAAP NGUA

SPICY BEEF SALAD

INGREDIENTS

- 175g (6oz) minced beef
- 2 teaspoons finely chopped galangal
- 2 tablespoons fish sauce
- 2 tablespoon lime juice
- 1 teaspoon sugar
- ½ teaspoon chilli powder
- 10 small shallots, thinly sliced
- 4 spring onions, finely chopped
- 2 teaspoon dry-fried rice (see page 10)
- 20 mint leaves
- A selection of raw crisp green vegetables, such as longbeans, morning glory and white cabbage

When I ate this dish in Laos, it was made with minced buffalo meat. Here I have substituted beef, less rich in flavour but certainly less chewy. You can vary the meat – chicken and pork would do, but my special favourite version uses minced Chinese roast duck.

In the original Laotian version, almost all the buffalo intestines and offal went into the mince, making it very nourishing. While I have stipulated plain beef mince here, you could be adventurous and add the liver, kidneys and heart if you wanted to get nearer to an authentic laap. In Laos the accompanying crisp green vegetables included young mango leaves, but these are unobtainable outside Asia, so use any fresh salad vegetables that are in season in your part of the world. This is another very piquant appetizer, which is good with drinks, though you can tone it down by serving it with sticky rice.

PREPARATION

Place the minced beef in a heavy-based saucepan and heat while stirring in the galangal, fish sauce, lime juice, sugar and chilli powder. Mix well until the meat is just cooked through. Remove from the heat and stir in the shallots, spring onions, dry-fried rice and mint leaves. Mix well. Turn out on a serving dish and serve with the selection of fresh crisp vegetables.

SAI UA MOO
PORK SAUSAGE

INGREDIENTS

- 10 garlic cloves
- 10 small shallots
- 10 black peppercorns
- 450g (1lb) minced pork (not lean pork: there should be about 20% fat)
- 1 teaspoon salt
- About 75cm (30in) of pigs' intestines
- Oil for deep-frying

TO SERVE:

- Lettuce or other fresh green leaves
- 4–6 small fresh red or green chillies
- Salted peanuts (optional)
- Fine matchsticks of fresh ginger (optional)

PREPARATION

In a mortar, pound the garlic, shallots and peppercorns to a paste. Turn this into a mixing bowl, add the minced pork and stir together. Add the salt, stirring well.

Pull the end of the intestine over the spout of a funnel and tie a knot at the far end of the tube. Force the mixture into the casing.

When there is 10cm (4in) of the mixture at the knotted end of the tube, tie a knot. Leave a small gap and tie a second knot. Continue stuffing and knotting until you have 5 or 6 sausages. If there are any air bubbles caught under the surface, prick them with a needle to release the air. Cut between the knots to separate the sausages.

The sausages should be deep-fried until a deep golden brown all over, then served with the fresh salad and the chillies to nibble on – you could also include salted peanuts and fine matchsticks of fresh ginger.

SOOP HOUA PHAK
COOKED VEGETABLE SALAD

INGREDIENTS

- 2 dried red chillies, soaked for 15 minutes then drained
- 6 small shallots
- 4 garlic cloves
- 4 hard-boiled eggs
- 2 tablespoons oil
- 2 tablespoons dried shrimp
- 1 tablespoon sesame seeds
- ½ teaspoon salt
- 115g (4oz) potatoes, finely diced
- 115g (4oz) cauliflower, cut into small florets
- 115g (4oz) longbeans, cut into 2.5cm (1in) lengths
- 115g (4oz) white radish, finely diced
- 175g (6oz) minced lean pork
- 2 tablespoons fish sauce
- 1 teaspoon sugar
- 2 tablespoons roasted peanuts
- A grinding of black pepper

PREPARATION

In a mortar, pound together the chillies, shallots and garlic to make a paste and set aside.

Shell the hard-boiled eggs. Separate the yolks, dice the whites and set both aside.

In a frying pan, heat the oil and fry the dried shrimp until crispy. Remove, drain and set aside.

In a dry frying pan, dry-fry the sesame seeds (see page 10) and set aside.

Fill a large pan with water and bring to the boil. Add the salt and the diced potatoes, bring back to the boil and cook for 5 minutes. Add all the other vegetables and boil briefly until they are just al dente. Drain and set aside.

Heat a dry wok and fry the minced pork, adding the fish sauce slowly to prevent sticking. Mix in the chilli paste and stir-fry until the pork is cooked through.

Add the egg yolks and sugar and stir well. Add the vegetables and diced egg whites, then stir well until everything is thoroughly coated. Turn out on a dish and serve sprinkled with the peanuts and pepper.

MOK PLA

FISH CURRY STEAMED IN BANANA LEAF

INGREDIENTS

- 6 small shallots
- 6 garlic cloves
- 2 dried red chillies, soaked for 15 minutes then drained
- 175g (6oz) fillets of cod or similar white fish
- 1 egg
- 3 tablespoons coconut cream
- 1 tablespoon fish sauce
- 20 holy basil leaves
- 1 whole banana leaf
- Toothpicks

PREPARATION

Preheat a hot grill. Place the shallots and garlic between two sheets of kitchen foil. Fold over the edges to seal and place this envelope under the hot grill. Cook, turning once, until the contents feel soft.

Unwrap the parcel and put the softened vegetables into a mortar together with the chillies. Pound to a paste.

Turn the paste into a mixing bowl, add the cod and break it up as you mix it with the paste. Break the egg into the bowl, add the coconut cream and fish sauce and stir well. Add the basil leaves, stir once and set aside.

You now need to make banana leaf 'envelopes' in which the mixture will be steamed (see the photograph on page 71). These containers will be pyramid-shaped and you will need two for this amount of filling. For each pyramid, cut out a rectangle of banana leaf, measuring roughly 30×15cm (12×6in). Round off the narrow ends to make a long oval shape. Place half the mixture at the centre of each, carefully easing up the long sides so that any liquid is held in and ensuring that these are slightly tucked in as you lift up. Bring together the rounded ends, squeezing them to a point which you fasten with a toothpick and which will give you your pyramid.
Go easy with the banana leaf which is fairly fragile and can simply crumble if forced too hard.

Place both pyramids in the upper compartment of a steamer and cook for 15 minutes. Each diner should have a pyramid which is opened at the table to release the pungent aroma of the steamed curry, which is scooped out and eaten in small amounts along with rice and other dishes.

KALEE PED

DUCK CURRY

INGREDIENTS

- 175g (6oz) duck breast, thinly sliced
- Salt and pepper
- 4 dried red chillies, soaked for 15 minutes then drained
- 6 small shallots
- 225ml (8fl oz) coconut cream
- 2 tablespoons fish sauce
- 1 teaspoon sugar
- 1 teaspoon Madras curry powder
- 225g (8oz) potatoes, cut into small cubes

PREPARATION

Season the duck with salt and pepper and set aside.

In a mortar, pound together the chillies and shallots to form a paste.

In a saucepan, heat the coconut cream and stir in the paste. Continue stirring until a rich aroma is given off, then add the seasoned duck and stir well. Now add fish sauce, sugar and curry powder and stir well. Add the potato cubes and stir well.

Cover and simmer until the potato cubes are cooked al dente – no more than 10 minutes. Turn out into a bowl and serve.

KAI JEUN NA SOM

SWEET-AND-SOUR FRIED EGGS

INGREDIENTS

- 2 tablespoons oil
- 6 eggs
- 115g (4oz) minced pork
- Salt and pepper to taste
- 60g (2oz) onion, cut into small dice
- 60g (2oz) tomato, cut into small dice
- 60g (2oz) sweet pepper, cut into small dice
- 60g (2oz) star-fruit or pineapple, cut into small dice
- 1 tablespoon sugar
- 1 tablespoon fish sauce
- 2 spring onions, finely chopped

PREPARATION

Heat the oil in a frying pan and fry 4 of the eggs, sunny-side up. Place on a serving dish and set aside. Reserve the frying oil in a bowl.

Next, in a large bowl, beat the 2 remaining eggs, stir in the minced pork and flavour to taste with salt and pepper.

Heat a wok or frying pan without any oil. Pour in the mixture and fry, stirring constantly so that it does not form into a patty. When the meat is just cooked through, remove and set aside.

Add the reserved oil to the wok or pan and reheat it. Fry the onion until golden. Add the tomato, sweet pepper, star-fruit or pineapple, sugar and fish sauce, stirring constantly. When well mixed, stir in the cooked pork and mix well.

Remove from the heat and stir in the spring onions. Pour over the fried eggs and serve.

KENG PLA
FISH SOUP

INGREDIENTS

- 2 eggs
- 2 tablespoons oil
- 1.2 litres (2 pints) pork stock (see page 14)
- 4 small shallots, thinly sliced
- 60g (2oz) black fungus mushrooms, soaked and drained (see page 19)
- 3 tablespoon fish sauce
- 115g (4oz) rice vermicelli, soaked and drained
- 175g (6oz) smoked haddock, broken into flakes
- 3 kaffir lime leaves, rolled into a cigarette shape and thinly sliced across into slivers
- A grinding of black pepper
- Coriander leaves to garnish

PREPARATION

In a bowl, beat the eggs lightly. Heat the oil in a flat frying pan, pour in the beaten eggs and fry to make a thin, firm, tortilla-like omelette. Remove and, when cool, cut into 5×0.5cm (2×¼in) strips and set aside.

In a large pan, heat the stock and add the shallots, mushrooms, fish sauce and vermicelli. Bring to the boil. Remove from the heat and add the omelette strips and the flaked fish. Stir well.

Add the kaffir lime leaf slivers and pepper, stir once and ladle into bowls. Garnish with coriander and serve.

YAM KAI TOM
BOILED CHICKEN SALAD

INGREDIENTS

- 175g (6oz) boneless chicken breast
- 2 garlic cloves, thinly sliced
- 5 small shallots, thinly sliced
- 2 small fresh red chillies, finely chopped
- 2 tablespoons fish sauce
- 2 tablespoon lime juice
- 1 tablespoon sugar
- 60g (2oz) cucumber, thinly sliced
- 2 medium tomatoes, cut into wedges
- 1 medium onion, thinly sliced and separated into rings
- 1 small lettuce, separated into leaves

PREPARATION

First boil the chicken in just enough water to cover for 10 minutes, until well cooked through. Remove from the pan and leave to cool, while continuing to boil the liquid to reduce it down to make a little concentrated stock, about 2 tablespoons only.

Meanwhile, in a bowl, prepare a dressing by mixing the garlic, shallots, chillies, fish sauce, lime juice and sugar, adding the 2 tablespoons of reduced chicken stock.

Place the salad vegetables in a large bowl. Skin the chicken and shred into the bowl. Pour over the dressing and mix thoroughly, then serve.

NGUA PAD MAK KHE UA
FRIED BEEF WITH AUBERGINE

INGREDIENTS

- 2 tablespoons oil
- 2 garlic cloves, finely chopped
- 4 small fresh red or green chillies, finely chopped
- 175g (6oz) minced beef
- 225g (8oz) aubergine, roughly sliced
- 2 tablespoon fish sauce
- 1 teaspoon sugar
- 20 sweet basil leaves

The original ingredients for this would be buffalo meat and an aubergine which would be one of the harder Oriental varieties rather than the large purple/black aubergine familiar in the West. However, I like this adapted version as much as the original and don't look on it as a poor substitute.

PREPARATION

Heat the oil in a wok or deep frying pan and fry the garlic until golden brown in colour.

Add the chillies and stir well. Add the minced beef, stir, then add the aubergine. Stir again, add the fish sauce and sugar, then stir-fry until the aubergine is just cooked through.

Add the basil leaves, stir thoroughly, then turn out on a dish and serve.

SOUSI PLA
SPICED COCONUT FISH

INGREDIENTS

- Oil for frying
- 1 medium trout, cleaned, filleted and cut into 5cm (2in) pieces
- 4 tablespoons coconut cream
- 2 tablespoons fish sauce
- 1 teaspoon sugar
- 4 kaffir lime leaves

FOR THE KHEUANG HOM (CHILLI PASTE):

- 3 dried red chillies, soaked for 15 minutes then drained
- 10 small shallots
- 4 garlic cloves

PREPARATION

First make the kheuang hom (chilli paste): in a mortar, pound together the, shallots and garlic to form a paste. Set aside.

In a wok, heat the oil and fry the trout pieces until golden, remove from the oil and set aside.

In a clean wok, heat the coconut cream, stirring well. Mix in the reserved chilli paste and simmer for a few seconds. Then add the fish sauce and sugar and stir. Add the fried fish and stir constantly until the pieces have absorbed some of the liquid but are not soft – this should take only a few seconds. Add the lime leaves, stir once, then serve.

KAI PAD MAK PHET DENG
FRIED CHICKEN WITH RED CHILLI

INGREDIENTS
- 225g (8oz) chicken, thinly sliced
- Salt and pepper
- 2 tablespoons oil
- 2 garlic cloves, finely chopped
- 1 onion, finely chopped
- 6 large fresh red chillies, sliced lengthways into slivers
- 8 spring onions, cut into 3.5cm (1½in) lengths
- 2 tablespoons fish sauce
- 1 teaspoon sugar
- Coriander to garnish

PREPARATION

Season the chicken pieces with salt and pepper to taste and set aside.

In a wok or deep frying pan, heat the oil and fry the garlic until golden brown in colour.

Add the seasoned chicken and stir-fry until almost cooked through. Stirring constantly, add all the remaining ingredients except the coriander and stir-fry until the chicken is cooked through.

Turn out on a dish, garnish with the coriander and serve.

PAD SOM SIN MOO
LEMON PORK

INGREDIENTS
- 2 tablespoons oil
- 20 small shallots, thinly sliced
- 175g (6oz) pork, cut into small thin pieces
- 2 tablespoons fish sauce
- 225ml (8fl oz) coconut milk
- 2 tablespoons lemon juice
- 1 teaspoon lemon rind, finely slivered
- 5 spring onions, cut into 2.5cm (1in) lengths
- Coriander leaves to garnish

PREPARATION

In a wok or deep frying pan, heat the oil and fry the shallots until golden brown and crispy. Set aside.

In the same hot oil, stir-fry the pork, adding the fish sauce. When the meat is just cooked through, add the reserved crispy shallots, stir, then add the coconut milk. Stir well, then add the lemon juice, lemon rind and spring onions. Stir well.

Turn out on a warmed serving dish and garnish with coriander leaves.

HED PAD SOM PHAK
MUSHROOMS FRIED WITH PICKLED CABBAGE

INGREDIENTS
- 2 tablespoons oil
- 2 garlic cloves, finely chopped
- 115g (4oz) firm mushrooms (oyster mushrooms, for example), coarsely chopped
- 175g (6oz) pickled cabbage (see page 15)
- 1 teaspoon sugar
- Salt and pepper

PREPARATION

Heat the oil in a wok or deep frying pan and fry the garlic until golden brown. Then add all the remaining ingredients and stir-fry briefly, for about 30 seconds, before turning out on a serving dish.

Because of the saltiness of the pickled cabbage you will need only a tiny amount of salt and pepper, so taste the dish before adding any.

NAM VAN LOI MAK TENG
MELON IN COCONUT MILK

INGREDIENTS
- 450ml (¾ pint) coconut milk
- 4 tablespoons sugar
- 175g (6oz) melon (not too ripe), cut into 1cm (½in) cubes
- Crushed ice

This dish is simplicity itself, but wonderfully refreshing on a hot day. The Asian melon is not very sweet, which provides a slight counterbalance to the sugary sauce, so this could be a good way to use up a not-too-ripe melon.

PREPARATION

In a saucepan, heat the coconut milk. Stir in the sugar, bring gently to the boil, then remove from the heat and leave to cool.

When cool, pour into a bowl and add the melon. Half-fill 2 individual dessert bowls with crushed ice, spoon over the melon and coconut milk and serve. If you do not have crushed ice, chill the mixture in the refrigerator before serving.

KHAO TOM MAK KUAY
STEAMED STICKY RICE WITH BANANA

INGREDIENTS
- 225g (8oz) sticky rice, soaked for 3–4 hours
- 500ml (16fl oz) coconut milk
- ¼ teaspoon salt
- 4 tablespoons sugar
- 5 small bananas, each about 10cm (4in) long, cut in half lengthways
- Banana leaves or kitchen foil

You often see these banana envelopes on sale at bus stops and railway stations. No one really knows their place of origin, but the use of sticky rice suggests that they may have started off in Laos. While taro and black beans are not uncommon, the small sweet banana remains the most usual filling. When I was a child we used to judge the sellers by how generous they were with the filling – those who tried to get four slices out of a banana were never patronized again.

PREPARATION

Drain the sticky rice and place it in a pan with the coconut milk. Bring to a simmer, stirring constantly, until the rice has just absorbed the liquid, about 5–10 minutes – at this point it will be half-cooked. Add the salt and sugar and stir in well, then remove from the heat and leave to cool.

Make 10 rectangles about 25×20cm (10×8in) out of banana leaf or kitchen foil. Scoop 2 tablespoons of half-cooked rice on to each rectangle, flatten gently and place a half-length of banana at the centre of each patty. Make an envelope by folding over first the long then the short sides.

Place, folded side down, in the upper compartment of a steamer and cook for ½ hour. Serve hot or cold.

Cambodia

BRIDESMAIDS IN PINK

At the end of the 12th century, the last great ruler of the Khmer empire, Jayavarman VII, built a new capital at Angkor Thom, about 3km north of the ancient temple complex of Angkor Wat. At the very heart of this walled domain, the king placed the Bayon, dedicated to the worship of the Hindu pantheon, with each of its 49 massive towers bearing 4 vast heads of the god Avaloketesvara. Today, those eerily smiling faces stare down at the awed spectators below as the huge structure shimmers out of the early morning mist blanketing the dense forest which has now engulfed what was once, with a million inhabitants, the largest city in the world.

Sculpted freeze, Angkor Wat

Despite the ravages of time and man, the Bayon still contains some of the greatest art ever made. Its stone walls are decorated with 1,200 metres of bas-relief carvings, in which over 11,000 figures enact scenes from Hindu mythology or heroic moments from the wars in which Jayavarman drove the invading Chams from the Khmer lands. Truly awesome in scale and complexity, these stories unfold like reels of film that run at three levels along the outer corridors of the complex. On the upper level, Jayavarman himself – much the largest figure – is depicted as Indra, King of the Gods, enthroned in a floating pavilion, watching over his victorious troops who can be seen on the next level down, suitably transformed into holy Devas as they drive away the Cham demons.

Yet for all this swirling activity, the scenes that most engage the passing observer are those running at eye level which depict a simpler world of everyday life: servants bringing up supplies and organizing the camp kitchens, where they are preparing food in ways remarkably similar to those that can be seen in rural Cambodia today. A cook is about to pitch a suckling pig into a boiling cauldron, two men are grilling fishes held in strips of bamboo, just as people still do all over Southeast Asia. Nothing changes – even as the great army marches home from its triumph, wagons creaking, elephants trumpeting, two men drop out by the side of the road to enjoy a bowl of rice.

In the past it was the scenes of military prowess that were held up as symbols of Cambodia's glorious past; today one could well take those more modest images of cooking and eating as an apt metaphor for life in the newly emerging nation, as it tries to recover from twenty years of abject misery. For the first-time visitor to the modern capital of Phnom Penh, one of the most striking things is the unexpected number of busy restaurants on its main thoroughfares and out along the banks of the Mekong, as it passes on its journey from Laos and Thailand to its estuary in Vietnam. Unexpected because all one seems to hear about the country are echoes of the horrors of 1975–9 and the agony of national destruction under the Khmer Rouge, and the subsequent Vietnamese invasion. Today, things are clearly far from stable and the tentative efforts to recreate a nation under an uneasy coalition of opposing groups may fall apart at any moment – and may well have done so before this book is published. At the time of writing, the country is again led by the aged King Sihanouk, who has controlled Cambodia's destiny since its declaration of independence from the French in 1953, save for a brief interlude when the Khmer Rouge took over the country. Today, Sihanouk is titular head of state, with the unenviable task of trying to hold together the opposing forces in the coalition, a task which appears to be undermining his health.

Politics aside, the country's main problems are the result of the unleashing of unbridled capitalism, fuelled by an influx of foreign investors which has given the once placid city something of the atmosphere of a frontier town. However, one only has to be taken, as I was, to the grim concrete school that Pol Pot used as his torture centre, to see that anything is preferable to that nightmare. After the school, I was driven out to the Killing Fields at Choeung Ek to see the mass graves and the high glass tower with its 8,000 skulls. As I stood in that terrible place I could hear the screams of the victims as if their souls hovered around the pitted ground. I hope they find peace some day.

Sadly the nightmare has not completely ended. Friends warned me not to travel too far from the main centres without armed protection against bandits and not to wander away from marked paths because of the countless land mines that are still scattered over much of the countryside. Having been told all these gloomy things, I was then driven across the new 'Japanese' bridge, along the Porimphorn Road on the banks of the Mekong, to the Hang Neak, one of a long line of large restaurants built on stilts above the river, its main room bedecked with winking fairy lights and loud with pop music.

When we got there we found a wedding party in progress, the bride in white lace, the groom somewhat stiff in his unfamiliar Western suit, the bridesmaids giggly in pink. As in the other countries of Southeast Asia, village people still have a traditional wedding in traditional dress, whereas city dwellers have two celebrations – a traditional wedding in the morning, followed by an early-evening party for which everyone changes into Western costume. Most people now wear simple Western clothes – trousers and shirts, loose dresses and blouses – for city life, though the combination of loose cotton top and wrap-around sarong for women, with baggy trousers for men, is still the preferred dress in farming communities.

Of course, young people want the latest American fashions and you see jeans and trainers everywhere. At another table in that restaurant there was a group of such teenagers enjoying Coca-Colas as a waitress lit the candles on a birthday cake covered in lurid red and green icing. And though it may appear tasteless to mention such things so close to the memory of torture and death, there is ample justification – frivolity is the best antidote to tyranny, innocent fun is the one thing no dictator can bear. The bustling restaurants of Phnom Penh are part of a healing process, a triumphant sign that the people of that ravaged land have a brighter future ahead of them, no matter what immediate problems they may encounter.

Twenty years of chaos have at least spared the city the destructive 'progress' of other Asian capitals. Phnom Penh still stretches languidly along the western bank of the Tonlé Sap river, just above the point where it meets the Mekong. The layout of the city is simple – two broad north-south avenues, crossed by five wide east-west boulevards. This simplicity has been somewhat spoiled by the recent renaming of many streets; the lords of communism, Marx and Lenin, have been pushed aside by the nation's monarchs – Monivong, Norodom and the present King Sihanouk. This tends to reinforce the first impression that Phnom Penh is a royal city and that its heart is the king's palace, above whose walls can be seen the spires of the silver pagoda and the throne hall and the burial stupas of the royal family.

The royal presence aside, Phnom Penh was really a French colonial creation, with wide tree-lined streets and handsome villas. Predominately ochre in colour, some are in Mediterranean stucco, others in the half-timbered Anglo-Norman style, so that from one street to the next the casual stroller moves effortlessly between Nice and Le Touquet. It is pleasing to note that Pol Pot's crazed attempt to obliterate all memory of the past by evacuating the city accidentally preserved a considerable amount of this colonial heritage, leaving far more of these lovely houses intact than can now be found in Vientiane. Happily, many of the newly arrived foreign businesses from Taiwan, Hong Kong, Bangkok and Tokyo are finding it congenial to establish their corporate headquarters in these attractive structures, offering some hope that the city may retain something of its former elegance.

In the twenties and thirties, when Art Deco, with its mix of European Modernism and folk elements from other cultures, became a universal style, the French graced Phnom Penh with an

Fishermen on Lake Tonlé Sap

imposing covered market in the new manner. The light is filtered through geometric latticework high in the curved roof of the shady central hall, from which radiate the long wings spread with stalls selling fabrics, electrical goods, household equipment and, of course, food. At first glance, the neat arrangements of lemon grass and mangosteen, of longbeans and star-fruit, look identical to food you can find in Thailand – a fair assumption when it turns out that much of what is on sale has indeed been imported from there. The Khmer Rouge not only destroyed buildings and Buddhas; they also wrecked the rural economy, closing traditional markets and turning peasant farmers into communal workers, a form of slave-labour that led to crop failure and starvation. The thoughtless scattering of land mines is still preventing a full return to normality, though the fact that the country may soon be able to export rice again says much about the resilience of ordinary people and of the country's potential for agricultural development, if a degree of political stability can be maintained and if the hidden land mines can be unearthed and disarmed.

While imports from Thailand temporarily fill the gap, village life is slowly returning to normal in those areas where the fighting has definitely ceased. Most families have communal land carefully squared-off and banked for flooding so that rice can be grown. Smaller plots are kept for vegetables like onions and morning glory

(water spinach), and chickens, both for eggs and the pot, all supplemented with some wild food: snakes and insects like ants and crickets. Where possible there is also a water buffalo for labour and ultimately for meat – tough but flavoursome. If there is any excess production, it can be sold at the nearest village market in exchange for herbs and spices to flavour the food.

At village level the main food eaten is plain boiled rice, with a little highly flavoured protein and vegetable to help it down. One meal is taken late morning at the point when the searing midday heat makes outdoor work impossible, a second in the early evening when the late afternoon tasks are done. Breakfast, at sun-up, is a case of eating any left-over rice from the night before, flavoured with other unfinished morsels. Of course, this is reversed in the city, where large amounts of meat – imported beef instead of buffalo – and elaborately prepared vegetable concoctions are preferred, not to mention a full American breakfast if possible.

In the city, Thai and Cambodian cuisines seem noticeably similar – as indeed do our two peoples – but the differences are just as important. Whereas we Thais migrated into the region, the Khmers have occupied what is today known as Cambodia since the beginning of recorded history and still make up 90 to 95 per

Village scene, central Cambodia

cent of the population, with a language and a form of writing as different from Thai as Latin is from ancient Greek. It is true that both countries share many similar basic dishes, often with very similar names, but a more careful examination reveals subtle differences, which in the case of Cambodian cookery is all to do with freshness and simplicity.

Thai cuisine today combines peasant cookery with the elaborate, highly flavoured dishes that were once the exclusive province of the high-born, many of which involve complicated cooking procedures and which produce a range of flavourings in the same dish. By contrast, Cambodian cookery is much simpler and relies more on the flavours of the original ingredients. The methods of cooking are often quite basic: quick stir-frying in a wok, steaming and simple grilling over a charcoal fire, leaving everything very fresh-tasting. It is rather like comparing French cuisine naturelle with the more complicated haute cuisine. In effect, the Cambodians have continued an older tradition of Southeast Asian cookery, a style that was common before the Portuguese brought the chilli from South America, when food was spiced with pepper and mustard seed to add sharpness without the burning harshness that chilli imparts.

The commonest flavouring put before diners in Cambodia is not chopped chillies in either rice vinegar or fish sauce, as it would be in Thailand or Laos, but tik marij, a mix of ground black pepper, salt and lime juice. Often the main course of a Cambodian meal is plainly cooked meat or fish with tik marij to flavour it, a pleasing combination of natural flavours with the pungent high notes from the sauce. This naturalness is further enhanced by the adoption of the Vietnamese tradition of serving crisp raw salads and vegetables as part of every meal – which seems French, but isn't.

As in Thailand and Laos, rice is the main staple, freshwater fish the primary source of protein, and fish sauce and pickled or fermented fish the most frequent forms of flavouring. The latter is also the basis for the second most usual dipping sauce, prahok, which caused some confusion at my first Cambodian meal at the Hang Neak restaurant, where the menu offered 'Beef with Cambodian Cheese'. This turned out to be slivers of beef that each diner grilled over a charcoal brazier brought to the table, after which the meat was dipped in the prahok sauce. This was the 'cheese', some over-literal French speaker having translated 'fermented' as 'fromage' which had in turn become 'cheese' in English. However it was translated, Saj Go Tik Prahok (page 99) was delicious. So too was a more direct adaptation of Cambodia's colonial heritage, the French baguette, which is still sold everywhere. This is used for making pork toasts, which in other Asian countries consists of small squares of bread with a little dollop of spiced minced pork on each, which are then deep-fried. In Cambodia this is blown up to gigantic proportions, with half a baguette covered in pork mince, and deep-fried a rich golden brown to make a meal in itself.

Overall, Phnom Penh was a far cry from the desolate and dangerous place some of my Thai friends had predicted, and their dire warnings about Angkor Wat were to prove even further from

Vietnamese sculpted heads, abandoned outside the Royal Palace, Phnom Penh

reality. When I flew north to Siam Reap, the little town near to the historical site, I found that it too was now bustling with new hotels and restaurants, though they are kept well away from the temples and palaces. The Samapheap Restaurant near the river offered a wide selection of Cambodian dishes, but my choice was to be regulated by my guide who insisted that the fish was much fresher than in the capital and so proceeded to order little else. He even sang the praises of the local sun-dried fish, which certainly had a rich savoury taste, duc I suspect to a greater addition of salt during the drying process than is usual elsewhere.

You can see fish being sun-dried all over Asia, by rivers up-country and along the beaches near the fishing villages on the coast. Any sort of small fish is suitable; they are cleaned, gutted, split open, salted and spread out on lattice frames for a day of direct tropical sunlight. They are taken in at dusk to protect them from night mist, then put out for a second day, which turns them golden brown, after which they can be hung in a shady place and kept for several months to be used as needed. In Siam Reap I ate the local variety in a hot-and-sour salad similar to the Thai yam but again with signs of Vietnamese influence in the addition of mint leaves and Chinese coriander – which has a broader leaf than the ordinary variety and tastes a little like celery.

An evening meal at the Bayon Restaurant on National Route 6 was much enlivened by a group of what I can only call 'drinks girls', each employed by one of the main brewers or distillers to promote their product and who come to your table hoping to get an order. There was 'Miss' Tiger Beer, 'Miss' Hennessy Cognac and others representing Coca-Cola, Johnny Walker, Angkor Beer and Heineken. As we were only five, one 'Miss' was left out and looked

**Faithful guardian of a ruined
shrine, Angkor Wat**

distinctly glum until one gentleman among us quickly downed his first drink and called her back to order another, thus making everyone happy.

I spent three days in Angkor doing what the French dubbed 'the Grand Circuit'. This is essential if one wants to get some notion of the scale and diversity of the Khmer golden age which spanned four centuries, alternating between Hinduism and Buddhism, with each successive ruler trying to outdo his predecessor with the size and splendour of his buildings. To the uninitiated, it comes as a surprise to realize that the ruins comprise more than the famous towered temples and include royal bathing pools and a gigantic parade ground. It was there that the king and his court stood on a long terrace, supported by carved elephants and the mythical bird, the garuda, to watch their armies marching past, just like the scenes recorded on the walls of the Bayon.

Although one begins with Angkor Wat itself, there is no sense of passing from best to least as the days unfold; each part of the tour offers its own unique delights. I was there in May at the beginning of the rainy season, which most tourists try to avoid. I in fact like the occasional monsoon-like downpour, which seldom lasts more than an hour each day and often creates spectacular effects of light and colour. When I first saw Angkor Wat, it had a stunning rainbow arched over its towers, and the Ta Prohm temple which I visited on the final day was greatly enlivened by a torrential downpour. Ta Prohm is the one temple that the French restorers, who had long debated the merits and demerits of rebuilding the fallen masonry, decided to leave pretty much as they found it. This allows the visitor to experience something of the thrill enjoyed by the first explorers when they cut their way through the undergrowth to find these amazing buildings caught in the destructive embrace of tendrils and creepers, the walls inextricably locked into the trunks and branches of giant banyan trees, strangling the carv-

**Monks receiving offerings of food
and other gifts during a festival**

ings and holding up the roofs and corridors. There is a feeling of dread as one clambers over the fallen stones and cowers under arches that are enmeshed in the branches of a tree that is itself dying, so that it is no longer possible to say what is holding up what. I had no sooner reached the heart of this sinister fortress than the light suddenly plunged to purple and violet and the rain began to ricochet off the tumbled lichened blocks like hissing gunfire. Sheltering in a darkened cloister, I knew I was sharing the place with bats and all manner of insects and perhaps even the deadly hannuman snake. The scene was grand opera and Hollywood all rolled into one and only needed the sudden appearance of Indiana Jones to complete the sense of unreality.

Back in Phnom Penh and with a Sunday to fill before flying back to Bangkok, I was advised to make the short journey out of town, to what the Cambodians call Koki Beach, for a rare culinary treat. I was not alone! Almost anyone in the city with access to transport, from government officials in their Mercedes to clerks on motor scooters, seemed to be making for this spot on the Mekong where whole families rent little stilt shelters in which to pass the day eating, drinking, talking and sleeping. They can buy their picnics from stalls selling everything from grilled chicken to deep-fried crickets. There is every kind of pickle; the fruit varieties such as mango are eaten as snacks, while others, like pickled garlic, are used as cooking ingredients. To finish, there was a delicious sweet made of sticky rice and coconut with fresh jackfruit grilled inside a banana leaf envelope (see page 104). Everyone was obviously enjoying their one precious day of leisure. For the older people it was clearly a memory of the way of life they had known before disaster struck and a hopeful sign that the healing process will continue and that their children, who splash about so innocently in the river, will never know anything else.

MUAN DOT

POT-ROASTED CHICKEN WITH LEMON GRASS

INGREDIENTS
- 1 small whole chicken
- 3–4 tablespoons oyster sauce
- 10 stalks of lemon grass
- Oil

TO SERVE:
- Tik Marij (see page 91)
- Tik Prahok (see page 94)

Having ordered what was listed as 'roast chicken' in a restaurant in Siam Reap, I was shown round an ovenless kitchen and wondered how they were going to 'roast' it and how they were going to do it quickly enough for our dinner. Even when I realized that they were about to pot-roast it in a covered wok I was still concerned about the time factor, though in the end my fears were groundless as the whole thing was achieved in a mere half-hour, yet the chicken was cooked through and delicious; a plump Western chicken will take slightly longer.

PREPARATION

Cover the chicken in the oyster sauce, inside and out, and leave to marinate for 30 minutes. Place the lemon grass in a heavy-based saucepan just big enough for the bird, and which has a tight-fitting lid, and add just enough oil to cover. Heat and, as the lemon grass begins to fry, place the whole chicken on top and cover with the lid. Pot-roast, turning every 15 minutes, until the chicken is cooked through, about 30 minutes to 1 hour depending on the size of the bird. It should be a rich golden-brown when cooking is complete, and the juices should run clear when the thickest part of the flesh is pierced. Discard the lemon grass, quarter the chicken and serve with both Cambodian sauces: Tik Marij and Tik Prahok.

CHAR BAI MREAH PRIU

EGG AND BASIL FRIED RICE

INGREDIENTS
- 2 tablespoons oil
- 2 small garlic cloves, finely chopped
- 2 long fresh red mild chillies, thinly sliced diagonally into ovals
- 115g (4oz) protein of choice (pork, chicken, seafood, etc), cut into small thin pieces
- 2 small eggs
- 225g (8oz) steamed rice
- 1 tablespoon fish sauce
- 1 tablespoon light soy sauce
- ½ teaspoon sugar
- 1 small onion, halved and thinly sliced
- 20 fresh holy basil leaves

This is the Cambodian variant of a basic one-dish meal found all over Southeast Asia. The nature of the main protein ingredient is left for the diner to choose. Elsewhere, egg fried rice and basil fried rice are two separate dishes; here they are brought together.

PREPARATION

Heat the oil in a wok or deep frying pan and fry the garlic until golden. Add the chillies, stir once, then add the protein of choice and stir-fry briefly until just cooked through. Break in the eggs and stir well. Add the rice and mix very well. Add all the remaining ingredients in turn, stirring once between each addition. Serve immediately.

CHAR MEE GANTANG
NOODLES WITH PORK AND EGGS

INGREDIENTS

- ½ teaspoon cornflour
- Lettuce leaves
- 4 tablespoons oil
- 175g (6oz) rice noodles, soaked if dried
- 2 garlic cloves, finely chopped
- 115g (4oz) pork, thinly sliced
- 1–2 ducks' egg(s) or 2–3 small hens' eggs
- 1 tablespoon fish sauce
- 1 tablespoon light soy sauce
- 1 teaspoon sugar
- 6 tablespoons pork stock or plain water
- ¼ teaspoon ground black pepper
- 115g (4oz) broccoli, coarsely chopped

This is another one-dish meal. The unusual thing is the abundant use of ducks' eggs – I was struck by the use of these large eggs when I visited Siam Reap, near Angkor Wat. There, I was told, a highly successful duck farm has resulted in a glut on the local market. They don't add much in terms of flavour and can be replaced with hens' eggs – but a large duck egg certainly adds body to a dish, as here.

PREPARATION

In a cup, mix the cornflour with a little water to make a thickening agent, and set aside. Arrange the washed and dried lettuce leaves on a serving dish and set aside.

Heat 2 tablespoons of the oil in a wok or deep frying pan and fry the noodles, stirring constantly, until warmed through. Remove from the oil and spread over the lettuce on the serving dish. Add the remaining oil to the wok or frying pan, then add the garlic and fry until golden brown. Add the pork and stir until just cooked through. Break in 1 of the ducks' eggs or 2 of the hens' eggs and stir well. Add the remaining ingredients in succession, stirring between each addition. When the broccoli is al dente, add the cornflour mixture and stir briefly to thicken the liquid. Pour the contents of the wok or frying pan over the noodles. For even extra body, you can fry 1 more egg and place it on top of the noodles before serving.

TIK MARIJ
CAMBODIAN PEPPER DIP

INGREDIENTS

- 4 teaspoons freshly ground black pepper
- 2 teaspoons salt
- 4 wedges of lime, sufficient to make 8 tablespoons of juice

This is usually placed in front of each diner at every meal. Limes are the indigenous citrus fruit of the region, lemons a more recent import and a poor substitute for the tangy zest of the little green native.

PREPARATION

Share the ingredients among 4 small dipping bowls (about the size of ramekin or individual soufflé dishes). Place a bowl before each diner. At the beginning of the meal everyone should squeeze the lime over the pepper and salt and stir until the salt dissolves. This dip is served at every meal for you to use at your discretion to sharpen the flavour of what you are eating, either by dipping a little food directly into the Tik Marij or by sprinkling a little over the rice on your plate.

SAMLOR JRUOH

HOT-AND-SOUR MUSHROOM AND TOMATO SOUP

INGREDIENTS

- 450ml (¾ pint) vegetable stock (see page 14)
- 5cm (2in) piece of lemon grass, coarsely chopped
- 3 kaffir lime leaves, coarsely chopped
- 5mm (¼in) piece of galangal, thinly sliced
- 1 large tomato, cut into wedges
- 115g (4oz) small whole straw mushrooms
- 3 tablespoons lime juice
- 2 tablespoons light soy sauce
- A pinch of salt
- 4–5 small fresh red or green chillies, broken open with a single blow from a spoon or pestle
- Coriander leaves to garnish

PREPARATION

In a large saucepan, heat the stock to a boil. Add all the ingredients except the coriander, bring back to the boil and simmer for 1 minute.

Transfer to a serving bowl, garnish with roughly torn coriander leaves and serve.

SAMLOR CHANANG DY

CLAY-POT BEEF, VEGETABLE AND NOODLE SOUP

INGREDIENTS

- 1 litre (1¾ pints) rich beef stock (see page 14)
- 2 ducks' or hens' eggs
- 225g (8oz) steak, thinly sliced
- 60g (2oz) each local seasonal quick-cooking vegetables of choice
- 60g (2oz) Chinese cabbage leaves, roughly sliced
- 60g (2oz) morning glory (water spinach)
- 2 spring onions, chopped into 2.5cm (1in) lengths
- 10–15 holy basil leaves
- 2 stems of coriander leaves
- 115g (4oz) egg noodles, soaked if dried
- 60g (2oz) beancurd sheet, soaked

This is party food. In Cambodia, a clay pot on a portable charcoal burner is brought to the table and inside is a succulent beef stock. Everyone will have their own tik marij (page 91) or tik prahok (page 94) to adjust the flavour to their own taste. A fondue set or a 'steam-boat heater' would make ideal substitutes for the clay pot, otherwise you'll just have to eat round a saucepan on the kitchen stove!

PREPARATION

First make rich beef stock as per the instructions on page 14. Let the stock cool and skim off any excess fat. Then either remove the bones and serve the stock with the other ingredients, or remove everything, pass the stock through a filter and serve as a clear liquid. Either way, reheat and place in a dish on a heater on the table.

Each diner is given a bowl and chopsticks and a second bowl with an egg (duck's or hen's). The egg is broken into the bowl, slightly beaten, and the pieces of steak dunked in it before being placed in the stock with whatever vegetables the diner chooses along with some herbs, noodles and beancurd. Cooking time is a matter of choice, though it will not be long before everyone is eating whatever they can pick out of the stock, enjoying everybody's additions with no complaint.

YOAM MAKAH TREY ANG

DEEP-FRIED SMOKED FISH WITH RAW MANGO SALAD

INGREDIENTS

- Enough lettuce leaves to cover a serving dish
- Oil for deep-frying
- 115g (4oz) smoked fish (Western smoked herring will do), cut across into thin slices
- 60g (2oz) raw green mango, finely chopped into matchsticks
- 30g (1oz) carrot, finely chopped into matchsticks
- 30g (1oz) onion, finely chopped
- 4–5 small fresh red or green chillies, finely chopped
- 2 tablespoons fish sauce
- 1–2 tablespoons lime juice (this is optional and depends on the flavour of the raw mango – if it is very sour, you won't need the lime juice)
- 1 teaspoon sugar
- 1 tablespoon coarsely chopped coriander leaf and stem
- Mint leaves to garnish

Yoam is the Cambodian equivalent of the Thai yam, the spicy salad often served as an appetizer with drinks. The smoked fish is especially good in northern Cambodia, near Angkor Wat.

PREPARATION

Arrange the lettuce leaves on a serving dish and set aside.

Heat the oil for deep-frying and deep-fry the fish until crispy. Remove from the oil and place in a mixing bowl. Add all the other ingredients except the mint. Stir well and turn out on the lettuce leaves.

Garnish with mint leaves and serve.

TIK PRAHOK

PICKLED FISH DIP

INGREDIENTS

- 1–2 tablespoons boiled fermented fish liquid (see right)
- 2 tablespoons lime juice
- 1 teaspoon sugar
- 2–4 small fresh red or green chillies, finely chopped
- 2.5cm (1in) piece of lemon grass (the young inner stem, after the hard outer layer has been peeled away), finely chopped
- 1 teaspoon very finely chopped coriander leaf and stem

This is the second of the basic Cambodian dipping sauces, though much less commonly served than tik marij, which always appears at meals.

As its basis, you will need to take from a jar of fermented or pickled fish (see page 14) a solid piece of fish with some liquid and place these in a saucepan. Remove any bones from the fish, then break up the flesh and mash with the liquid. Bring gently to the boil, and simmer for a few moments to kill off any impurities. Allow to cool, then taste – if it is very salty, you will need to use only 1 tablespoon for this recipe; if not, then up to 2 tablespoons will be needed.

PREPARATION

Place all the ingredients in a mixing bowl and stir well. Transfer to a single serving dish or to smaller individual dipping dishes.

TROP BAMPORNG JIAMUAY PONG TIA
FRIED AUBERGINE WITH EGG

INGREDIENTS

- 2 large ducks' eggs or 4 medium hens' eggs
- 1 large whole purple aubergine, sliced across into thin rounds
- 3 tablespoons oil
- 1 tablespoon fish sauce (soy sauce if vegetarian)
- A grinding of black pepper
- ½ teaspoon sugar
- 2 medium spring onions, finely chopped

PREPARATION

Break 1 of the ducks' eggs or 2 hens' eggs into a mixing bowl and beat. Add the aubergine slices and coat well in the egg.

Heat 2 tablespoons of the oil in a wok or deep frying pan and fry the coated aubergine slices until golden and crispy. Remove from the oil and set aside.

Add the remaining tablespoon of oil to the pan, heat and break in the remaining egg(s). As they begin to cook, add the fish sauce, pepper and sugar and stir to blend them with the egg.

Then quickly add the fried aubergine rings and the spring onions, covering them with the scrambled egg. Allow to cook to the consistency of a Spanish omelette. When browned on the underside, turn over and cook the other side.

Transfer to a dish and serve.

OP JUMNEE JRUK BAMPORNG
SWEET-AND-SOUR SPARE RIBS

INGREDIENTS

- 275g (10oz) pork spare ribs from a young pig, chopped into 2.5cm (1in) lengths
- Salt and pepper to taste
- 4 tablespoons oil
- 115g (4oz) fresh pineapple segments
- 2 medium tomatoes, cut into wedges
- 2 large spring onions, coarsely chopped
- 2 tablespoons fish sauce
- 1 tablespoon lime juice
- 2 teaspoons sugar
- 2 tablespoons chicken stock or plain water
- A grinding of black pepper
- Coriander leaves to garnish

PREPARATION

Coat the spare ribs with salt and pepper. Heat the oil in a wok or deep frying pan and fry the spare ribs until golden brown on all sides. Remove from the oil and set aside.

Place the pineapple, tomatoes and spring onions in the hot oil, stir briefly, then add all the remaining ingredients except the coriander. Stir briefly and pour over the spare ribs,

Garnish with coriander leaves and serve.

SAJ GO TIK PRAHOK
BEEF AND RAW VEGETABLES WITH PICKLED FISH DIP

INGREDIENTS
- Tik Prahok (see page 94)
- A selection of raw vegetables, such as longbean, green aubergine, white cabbage and plantain banana
- 225g (8oz) good-quality beef steak
- A piece of pork fat or a cube of lard

This is a dish that I ate at the Hang Neak Restaurant on the banks of the Mekong, while the wedding party was under way. The Cambodians use a special piece of equipment on which the beef is seared, which is not unlike an upturned colander placed over a charcoal grill. It would be possible to improvise something like this over a barbecue, but one of those thick French griddle plates will achieve much the same effect.

PREPARATION

First prepare a bowl of Tik Prahok (see page 94).

Wash and prepare the vegetables according to type: quarter the round aubergines, break up the cabbage into leaves, peel and dice the plantain, etc. Arrange on a serving dish and set aside. Slice the beef into thin slivers.

Preheat a Cambodian grill or a griddle plate. Draw a piece of pork fat or a cube of lard over the cooking surface. When it sizzles, lay strips of beef all over the surface and cook, turning once.

When cooked to taste, lift away, dip into the Tik Prahok sauce and eat with the raw vegetables.

Alternatively, place the whole piece of steak under a very hot grill and sear one side. Turn, sear the other side. Remove, slice thinly and serve.

PLEA SAJ GO
HOT-AND-SOUR BEEF SALAD

INGREDIENTS
- Enough Lettuce leaves to cover a serving dish
- 225g (8oz) tender beef steak
- 2 tablespoons fish sauce
- 2 tablespoons lime juice
- 1 teaspoon sugar
- 1 onion, halved and sliced
- 4–5 small fresh red or green chillies, finely chopped
- 20 chilli leaves (these are hard to find outside Asia; the same amount of mint leaves may be substituted)

PREPARATION

Cover a serving dish with washed and dried lettuce leaves and set aside.

Grill the steak to taste – for authenticity you should leave it very rare. As you grill it, catch the juices in a dish. Quickly slice the steak very thinly, again retaining any juices.

Put the steak and all the juices into a mixing bowl, add the fish sauce and lime juice and mix well. Add all the other ingredients in turn, stirring once between each addition.

After adding the chilli or mint leaves, turn quickly out on the lettuce and serve while still warm.

SAMLOR TIK TUMPEANG
FISH, COCONUT AND YOUNG BAMBOO SHOOT SOUP

INGREDIENTS

- 1 teaspoon whole white peppercorns
- 5 small shallots, coarsely chopped
- 450ml (¾ pint) coconut milk
- 1 teaspoon tamarind water (page 19) or 1 tablespoon lime juice
- 1 tablespoon fish sauce
- 1 teaspoon sugar
- 115g (4oz) young bamboo shoots, boiled for 20 minutes, or raw green asparagus, chopped into 5cm (2in) pieces
- 2 small whole fish (good-sized sardines or small herrings would do), cleaned and gutted, topped and tailed and cut in half
- 225ml (8fl oz) vegetable stock (see page 14)

Despite the use of the word samlor, this dish and the Samlor Chanang Dy on page 93 are not so much soups as just very liquid dishes. This is really a curry and shouldn't be spooned up on its own, but poured over rice and then eaten.

Ideally it should be made with fresh young bamboo shoots, boiled for about 20 minutes. As these are virtually impossible to find in the West, however, and as canned bamboo shoots are usually quite old, you might prefer to use fresh asparagus to give a result closer to the original.

PREPARATION

In a mortar, pound the peppercorns, add the shallots and pound together to form a paste. Set aside.

In a saucepan, heat the coconut milk, add the pepper-and-shallot paste and simmer gently for 1 minute. Add the tamarind water or lime juice, fish sauce and sugar and stir.

Add the bamboo shoots or asparagus and simmer briefly. Add the pieces of fish and the stock, return to the boil, then reduce the heat and simmer very briefly, taking care that the fish does not break up.

When the fish is cooked through, turn out into a bowl and serve.

TREY PRAMAR JAMHOY
OMELETTE WITH PORK AND PICKLED FISH

INGREDIENTS

- 2 ducks' eggs or 3 large hens' eggs
- 60g (2oz) minced pork
- 1 teaspoon fermented or pickled fish liquid (see page 14)
- 2 tablespoons oil

FOR THE RAW VEGETABLE SIDE DISH:

- 1 small onion, cut into rings
- 7.5cm (3in) piece of cucumber, sliced
- 1 tomato, cut into wedges
- 2 stems of holy basil

PREPARATION

First make the side dish: mix together all the ingredients and turn into a serving dish. Set aside.

Beat the eggs well in a bowl. Add the minced pork and fermented fish liquid and mix well.

Heat the oil until smoking. Quickly pour in the egg mixture and let it rise. When the underside begins to brown, turn it over and repeat the process

Serve the omelette with the raw vegetable side dish.

AAMOH

STEAMED FISH CURRY

INGREDIENTS

- 1 tablespoon curry paste as used for Muan Char Kreung (see page 103)
- 225g (8oz) fish (roughly 1 medium-sized river trout)
- 1 tablespoon fish sauce
- 1 teaspoon sugar
- 1 large egg
- 3 tablespoons coconut cream
- Salt and pepper to taste
- 4 kaffir lime leaves, rolled into a cigarette shape and thinly sliced

This is the Cambodian version of the steamed curry dish found across Southeast Asia, similar to the Thai dish haw muk. Ideally, aamoh is served inside a fresh green coconut, so that the soft sweet flesh of the nut can be scraped out and eaten with the curry. If you can't find a fresh young coconut, serve in the steamer bowl. The following measurements will fill one coconut or one medium-sized bowl.

PREPARATION

First make the same curry paste as used for Muan Char Kreung (see page 103).

Top and tail the fish, cut open lengthways, fillet, then slice across into 2.5cm (1in) pieces.

Place the fish pieces in a medium-sized bowl and add all the other ingredients. Using your fingers, knead into a smooth paste.

Place the bowl in the top compartment of a steamer and steam until cooked, about 10 minutes (test by inserting a skewer, which should come out dry).

Either scrape the steamed curry into a young green coconut or serve in the steaming bowl.

LOCLAC

STIR-FRIED PORK WITH SALAD AND TIK MARIJ

INGREDIENTS

- Tik Marij (see page 91)
- A selection of seasonal salad vegetables, such as lettuce, tomatoes and onions
- 225g (8oz) pork fillet, thinly sliced into 2.5cm (1in) strips
- Salt and pepper
- 2 tablespoons oil

This is a very easy dish to make but, as it is accompanied by the classic Cambodian dip, it has all the authentic flavours of the country's cuisine. This could be served as a snack or as party-food; or, if part of a main meal, it could then be brought out early as an appetizer, or served with drinks in the Thai manner.

PREPARATION

First prepare the Tik Marij (see page 91). Slice the seasonal salad vegetables and arrange on a serving platter. In a mixing bowl, generously season the pork slices with salt and pepper.

Heat the oil in a wok or deep frying pan and stir-fry the seasoned pork until browned all over and just cooked through. Turn out on the salad and serve with the Tik Marij.

MUAN CHAR KREUNG
CHICKEN FRIED WITH CURRY PASTE

INGREDIENTS
- 2 tablespoons oil
- 225g (8oz) thinly sliced chicken pieces
- 1 tablespoon prepared curry paste
- 2 tablespoon fish sauce
- 1 teaspoon sugar
- 1 tablespoon ground roasted peanuts
- 1 medium sweet pepper, cut into thin strips

FOR THE CURRY PASTE:
- 2.5cm (1in) piece of galangal, peeled and finely chopped
- 1 tablespoon finely chopped lemon grass
- 1 teaspoon lime rind, finely chopped
- 5 large dried red chillies, soaked in water for 30 minutes, then split open, deseeded and finely chopped
- 1 teaspoon salt

This is another dish from the Samapheap Restaurant near Angkor Wat. The curry paste that you will make for this recipe is also needed for the dish Aamoh on page 101, so you may wish to make double the amount. It will keep in a refrigerator for at least a week.

PREPARATION
First make the curry paste: in a mortar, pound all the ingredients together to form a paste. Set aside.

In a wok or deep frying pan, heat the oil. Add the chicken pieces, stir and add the curry paste. Stir well, then add the other ingredients in succession, stirring once between each addition.

The sweet pepper should barely be in the oil for a moment before you turn everything out on a dish to serve.

MUAN CHAR KHYEY
CHICKEN WITH GINGER

INGREDIENTS
- 2 tablespoons oil
- 225g (8oz) chicken, thinly sliced
- 2 tablespoons oyster sauce
- 5cm (2in) piece of ginger, peeled and cut into fine matchsticks
- 1 teaspoon sugar
- 3 medium spring onions, chopped into 2.5cm (1in) lengths
- A sprinkling of ground black pepper
- 2–3 tablespoons chicken stock (see page 14) or plain water

PREPARATION
In a wok or deep frying pan, heat the oil and briefly fry the chicken, adding the oyster sauce and turning to coat well.

Add all the other ingredients except the stock, stirring constantly. If the mixture appears too dry, add a little chicken stock or water occasionally.

As soon as the chicken is cooked through, remove from the heat and serve.

BAI DAMNERB GRUOP KHANO
GRILLED STICKY RICE WITH COCONUT AND JACKFRUIT

INGREDIENTS

- 1 banana leaf
- 275g (10oz) cooked sticky rice, preferably still warm
- 225ml (8fl oz) coconut milk
- 2 tablespoons sugar
- ½ teaspoon salt
- 60g (2oz) coconut scrapings
- 115g (4oz) jackfruit, coarsely chopped into small pieces
- Toothpicks

This delicious pudding, which I found at Koki Beach, outside Phnom Penh, needs to be grilled inside banana leaf. While this can now be found in the West, you will probably have to buy more than you need here, so look around this book for other recipes that need some. Fresh jackfruit are unlikely to be easily available in the West but tinned segments would do here.

PREPARATION

First cut the banana leaf down either side of the central stem. Discard the stem, set aside one half of the leaf and cut the other into 8 strips, roughly 10cm (4in) wide. Set aside.

In a large bowl, mix the sticky rice with the coconut milk, sugar and salt. Leave to cool and dry (in a cool climate this should take no more than 30 minutes). Roll this mixture into 8 balls and place one on each section of banana leaf. Add to each an equal amount of coconut scrapings and jackfruit. Fold over 2 opposite corners of the leaf section, then fold the 2 remaining corners and pin with a toothpick to make a sealed envelope.

Preheat a moderate grill. Place the 8 envelopes under the grill and cook, turning from time to time, until the leaf envelopes begin to blacken.

Remove, open each envelope and serve the grilled rice balls with jackfruit on the open leaf, either hot or cold (see the photograph on page 105).

MEE CHAR
VEGETARIAN EGG NOODLES

INGREDIENTS

- 2 tablespoons oil
- 2 small garlic cloves, finely chopped
- 1–2 small dried red chillies, coarsely chopped
- 85g (3oz) or 1 nest of egg noodles (see page 11), soaked if dried
- 1 tablespoon dark soy sauce
- 1 tablespoon light soy sauce
- ½ teaspoon sugar
- 60g (2oz) beansprouts
- 60g (2oz) broccoli, cut small
- 60g (2oz) carrot, cut into fine matchsticks
- Coriander leaves to garnish

Those vegetarians who do not eat eggs need not worry: egg noodles are no longer what they were – the yellow colour comes from vegetable dye. If the name still causes concern, however, simply substitute some other white noodle.

PREPARATION

In a wok or deep frying pan, heat the oil and fry the garlic until golden brown. Add the chillies and stir well. Next, add all the remaining ingredients in succession except the coriander, stirring once between each addition.

Mix well, turn out on a serving dish and garnish with the roughly separated coriander leaves.

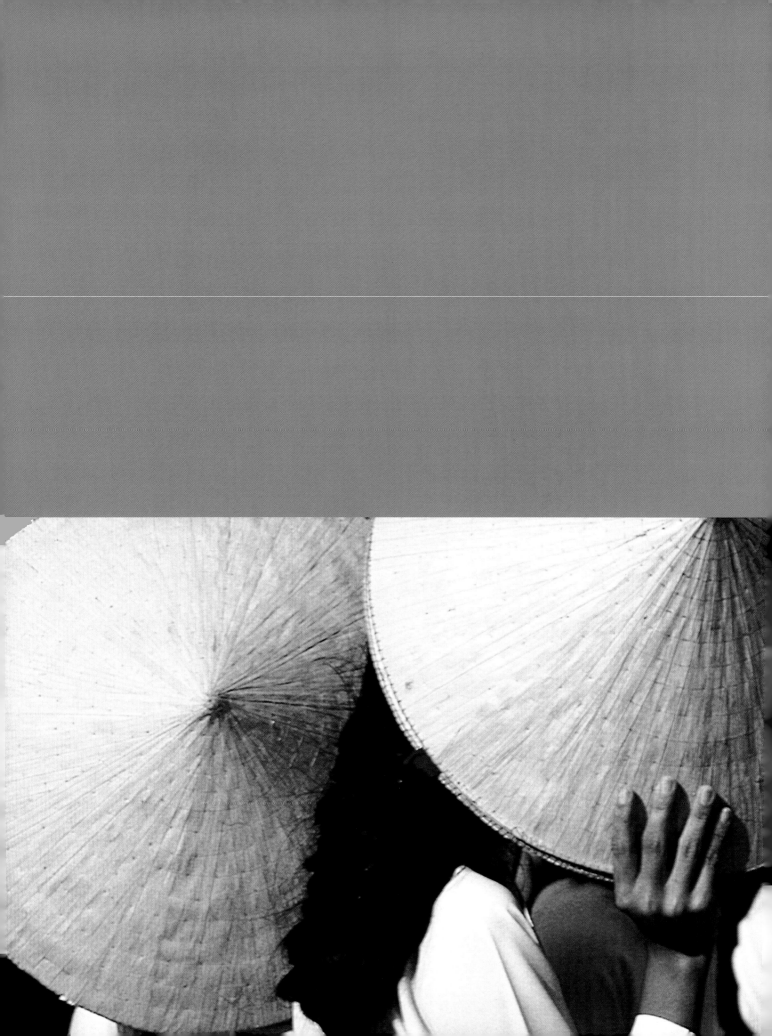

Vietnam

A MILLION BICYCLES

Even before you land at Hanoi's Noi Bai airport you can see how different Vietnam is from the rest of Southeast Asia. From the air, the squared-off pattern of rice-fields and irrigation canals looks much the same, but closer in the concrete houses, with their dipped tiled roofs curled at the edges, seem unmistakably Chinese. This is the first evidence of the influence on Vietnam of its powerful northern neighbour. Though the two lands were often at war, contact was constant and profound, reinforced today by the shared experience of communism. Inevitably, it is this recent past, and in particular the war with the United States, that conditions our image of Vietnam and was why I wanted, above all, to visit the North, which has been open to the outside world only since about 1991.

**Novice monks repairing
a temple roof**

When I arrived it was hard to be sure whether there really were so many soldiers at the airport or whether I was just imagining them. Everyone seemed to be in uniform and all around I could see a yellow star on a bright red background, on flags and badges and posters. It all seemed strangely familiar – *The Deer Hunter, Apocalypse Now, Good Morning, Vietnam* – no one can visit the country with an open mind; everyone has shared its terrible history.

I had been warned about the bureaucracy at the airport – the forms to be filled in and the risk of fines or worse if one tries to leave the country without having obtained the correct stamps on arrival. In the end someone must have decided to simplify the procedure and I was waved through with barely a glance, though my entire stay was overshadowed by the fear that I'd done something wrong and would pay for it later.

Such worries are not entirely unjustified. There are real tensions within the country: some old, like the ancient rivalry between North and South; others new, caused by the struggle between factions eager for their country to join the rest of modern Asia, who are in conflict with older figures still ruling from the capital city of Hanoi.

The hotel had sent a car, even more decrepit than the classic vehicles I had seen in Vientiane. It proved a bumpy journey along the surprisingly long road into the capital, though at least there were the rice farms with their 'Chinese' houses to take my mind off the discomfort. Here was a land that had held at bay the world's greatest industrial power, yet I could see two figures, wearing the classic white shell hats, swinging water from one ditch to another in a woven basket held by two ropes. Despite this simplicity, I knew that the country was well on the way to becoming a net exporter of rice and coffee, a target since achieved and stunning evidence of the skill and sheer hard work of these incredibly tenacious people. The main error the communists made was to interfere with the system of distribution. Produce could not get to market and only a decade ago the country collapsed into famine. Thankfully, that was now over and I was looking forward to seeing how far the food supply had returned to normal, a key factor in any study of a nation's cooking.

It was easy to see why the rice-fields were such a rich emerald green. I'd been warned about the notoriously bad weather in the uplands of North Vietnam and had tried, unsuccessfully it turned out, to visit the country at the opening of the dry season. As ill-luck would have it, I was to find Hanoi under a thin cold sheen of highland mist that lasted throughout my stay. It affected everything: my hotel was damp and unheated and none too clean; another possibility about which I had been warned, but which was still depressing. At least it was only a short walk to the Old Quarter, a jumble of narrow streets named, in medieval fashion, after the trades practised there: Rice Street, Fish Street, etc. Any manufactured goods looked noticeably cheap and gaudy, revealing their origins in fraternal communist countries – large aluminium vacuum flasks, bright red plastic shoes. More surprisingly, people seemed to live on the streets, washing by the side of the road, turning the pavements into living rooms – evidence of the notorious over-crowding and lack of amenities in the badly maintained urban areas. You can even see open-air massage parlours and roadside barbers' shops, almost everything down to sculptors carving gravestones, adding whatever image the family requires: Jesus, a pop star, even Ho Chi Minh, if you wish.

I decided to look into a tiny street-side temple, a miniature Chinese shrine where a small antechamber filled with plants led to an equally tiny, darker inner room with an altar and an alcove with three Chinese deities and a second altar with a statue to the Goddess of Mercy. She is a very powerful figure in the Chinese pantheon and revered by many Buddhists in Asia. Having made her an offering of incense, I was immediately rewarded on leaving the temple with the sight of a woman on the pavement opposite, kneeling beside a charcoal burner, frying banana fritters in a wok. This is a common enough sight all over the region. The banana slices are dipped in a batter made of rice flour and coconut milk, then deep-fried. This time, however, there was an interesting variation: the woman was also frying battered sweet potato, measuring out a portion by placing two slices of battered banana side by side on her shovel-spatula, crossing these with two slices of battered sweet potato, then lowering them into the hot oil. I bought a portion, neatly wrapped in newspaper, and walked on, happy to have taken a first step into the world of Vietnamese cooking.

I had already been warned that my visit might not be one of

Statue of the Emperor Khai Dinh in his mortuary complex outside Hué

the great eating experiences of my life. The guidebooks were unanimous that while some noodle stalls and other fast-food eating places had survived, many restaurants in the North had closed down in the years immediately following the end of the war, and were only now beginning to re-open. While I have eaten Vietnamese food in other countries, I have always wondered how authentic it was. There are many Vietnamese restaurants in France, but they appear to have been opened by Vietnamese-Chinese, later immigrants from China who settled in Vietnam during the colonial era, before moving on to different parts of the French Empire, or to France itself. Many of them opened restaurants that offered the sort of mix of Chinese and Vietnamese cooking that they and the colonial officers and their families liked to eat.

While this style of cooking contains genuine Vietnamese elements, it is basically Chinese. Everything is usually cooked in a

The statues of mandarins standing guard in the Salutation Court at the entrance to Khai Dinh's tomb

wok and there is a tendency to employ quite thick sauces. By contrast, the sort of food served by later refugees who passed through Laos, over the Mekong into Thailand, is much fresher, relying more on raw salads and vegetables and on the sort of light, last-minute cooking and grilling over charcoal that is common in the rest of Southeast Asia. I had already eaten wonderful meals in restaurants in Northeastern Thailand, in Nong Khai and Udon. While some of those dishes were bound to have been influenced by the demands of Thai customers, there was nevertheless a greater sense of balance between cooked and raw that seemed somehow more genuine.

It is a balance that grows out of the country's history. One of the original groups to occupy the thin coastal strip that is modern Vietnam were the Chams, whom we last saw being roundly defeated on the Angkor carvings. They were nudged aside by the ancestors of today's Vietnamese who, in turn, were heavily influenced by waves of Chinese invaders attempting to gain control of the strategic Red River Delta, where modern Hanoi now stands. The result, in terms of food, is a split between North and South. Northern food is more Chinese, with influences from neighbouring Laos in the use of galangal and with grilling over charcoal, which is not a feature of Chinese cuisine. By contrast, southern food shows the influence of Cambodia in the use of chillies and shrimp paste, to create flavours that are closer to those of the food of other countries in Southeast Asia.

The particular feature of all Vietnamese food, of both North and South, is perhaps texture – the use of al dente vegetables, like beansprouts, with nuts and other fresh or uncooked vegetables and herbs (another non-Chinese element) to give a dish a springy

or a crunchy edge. Two other practices have a significant effect: far less sugar is used than elsewhere in the region, and far more mint. There is a unique Vietnamese mint (see page 16) which has hints of coriander and which turns up – always uncooked, otherwise it is too dominant – in a whole range of dishes. To imagine the general taste of Vietnamese cooking you would have to combine the salty savouriness of Chinese cuisine with the sort of fish and lemon/lime flavours you get in Thai, Laotian and Cambodian food. Two of the most typically Vietnamese dishes highlight these unions: the classic nem, an unfried spring roll served with of fresh salad and heavily flavoured with Vietnamese mint, which is Lao in style; and, second, the classic Vietnamese noodle dish pho, which is clearly Chinese in origin. The French presence tended to encourage the Chinese side of Vietnamese cuisine, along with effecting the introduction of the baguette and some forms of pâté and sausage-making.

As you wander out of the Old Quarter, memories of that colonial past still linger in the part of town once reserved for senior French officials and leaders of the colonial business community, whose mansions far exceed anything on show in Vientiane or Phnom Penh. These imposing ochre Mediterranean villas are set back from wide tree-lined boulevards that radiate out from the large park at whose centre is the vast Governor's Residence. Now the Presidential Palace and looking not unlike a rather ornate fin-de-siècle grand hotel, this was once the heart of France's dream of a mighty Indo-Chinese Empire to rival British India. As if to show his contempt for such pretensions, Ho Chi Minh, leader of Vietnam's struggle for independence, refused to occupy the palace, choosing instead to live in a simple wooden stilt-house nearby. But such modesty did not long outlast Ho's death in 1969, and today his corpse, carefully maintained by an annual visit to a special embalming centre in Russia, now lies under glass in a mighty stone mausoleum. A visit is an eerie experience for those willing to brave the long shuffling queues, past scowling female guards, up chilly marble stairways, to the dimly lit hall where his curiously sallow cadaver awaits.

At the nearby army museum there is a grim display of captured guns, planes and tanks from the various wars the country suffered, first with the French and later the Americans. A room in the museum is set out like a theatre, with a large model of the valley at Dien Bien Phu where the French army was devastatingly overwhelmed in 1954. Lights pick out the points where the battles were fought, while video screens show newsreel footage of the events as they progressed towards the inevitable humiliating surrender. As I watched these flickering images, I gradually realized that my fellow spectators were all speaking French, pointing out events as they happened, involved in the whole thing in a way that made it obvious that they were veterans of the battle, come back from France to relive those terrible experiences of 40 years earlier.

Having explored some of the tourist sites, I now decided to follow my usual routine by visiting the main market. For this, I took one of the famous 'cyclos', bicycles with seats at the front in which terrified passengers are propelled into packed traffic by the pounding legs of a nerveless chauffeur, who takes little notice of which side of the road should be used. These cyclo drivers are said to have a terrible existence, exploited by the loan-sharks who

actually own the bikes, often weighed down with impossible loads so that it is no surprise to learn that they are the main customers of the roadside massage parlours. A single light-weight passenger like me must be something of a relief.

We quickly found the famous Don Xuan market, or at least what was left of it, for, as I now learned, the huge complex of halls that had sheltered hundreds of stalls, where over 3,000 people were employed, had burned down the previous year. Temporary stalls had sprung up in the surrounding streets, making it the one part of Hanoi that had some of the anarchic bustle and noise one expects in a major Asian city. While this was nothing like the vast spectacle the old market must have presented, at least I could get some idea of the scale of what was on offer. Interestingly, this appeared to fit in with my belief that Vietnamese food is more Southeast Asian than one would guess from what is often served abroad. The piles of lemon grass and tamarind, and the huge heaps of coconuts, would have been of little use for Chinese-style cooking, while the presence of galangal and jars of the Vietnamese version of fermented fish, mam nem, showed the clear influence of the eating habits of neighbouring Laos.

My aim now was to consume some of these things, and a mix of broken English and sign language conveyed to the cyclo driver my desire to find a restaurant. In the end we trotted up to a main eating area, with a line of noodle shops, each with a stove at the front where the cook was either dunking his ingredients in boiling water or stir-frying them in a wok. I picked the largest and busiest and squatted down on a low stool at a low table, an uncomfortable compromise between sitting up in the Western way or down on the floor in traditional style. Deciding to stick with what I assumed was local custom, I ordered Pho Ga Hanh Xao, a noodle soup made with chicken and crispy shallots (see page 119), very comforting in that drizzly climate. However, as I ate, I could see that, unlike most Chinese-style noodle shops, this place had a rear kitchen where other foods were being prepared. I could even see meat cooking on a charcoal grill, which is definitely not Chinese. Keen to try, I ordered a side dish of spare ribs deep-fried with chilli and lemon grass – xa suon chao – obviously Southeast Asian, as was the lime dip that accompanied it, which turned out to be the same as the tik marij I'd discovered in Cambodia.

The next day I left for Hué, the former capital, halfway down the country, almost midway between Hanoi and Ho Chi Minh City (the former Saigon). This is where most of the nation's cultural treasures are to be found and after Hanoi the old city is pure pleasure, not least because the Century Riverside Inn is modern, clean, dry and well run. As its name implies, the hotel stands on the Perfume River just above the point where it begins to divide into tributaries on the remainder of its 16-kilometre journey to the South China Sea. This pleasant location, at the very centre of the country, makes it easy to see why the Nguyen dynasty, the last emperors of Vietnam, chose Hué as their capital. Sadly, history has not proved so generous – the city and the Imperial Palace were

Selling fish, Hoi An

Mask seller, Hanoi

bombarded and occupied in turn by the French, the Viet Cong and the Americans, leaving only a fraction of its cultural treasures intact.

The hotel is on the bank of the river, where the new or 'European' town was built, while on the opposite side are the remains of the Purple Forbidden City, the walled and moated enclosure that was the private domain of the Imperial family. This was modelled on the Forbidden City in Beijing, and had the same series of interlinked courtyards and pavilions reserved for the Emperor, his Empress and his mother, with only a few buildings, such as the throne hall, accessible to ambassadors from the outside world. Most of the palaces and halls were utterly destroyed in 1968 in the aftermath of the Tet Offensive, when the American and South Vietnamese forces attempted to dislodge the Viet Cong who had carried out a horrendous blood bath after occupying the city. Today, UNESCO is gradually restoring the buildings with great care, starting with the outer gate-houses, so that it is possible to see something of the sumptuous red and gold carvings, the gilded furnishings and the jade and silver ornaments that lay hidden behind the high blank walls and which must once have rivalled their original inspiration in China.

The last Imperial family, the Nguyen dynasty, only came to power as late as 1802 and had hardly unified the country before the French began to meddle in their affairs. To see something of their brief rule one must recross the river and travel out to the hills beyond the new town, to where each succeeding Emperor built himself a fabulous tomb in order to ensure his worship and thus his repose for eternity. All the tombs are different and the most highly regarded are those that display a subtle integration of buildings and landscape, with walkways and terraces interlaced with lakes and pagodas. I have to admit, however, to liking best the one that the experts most denigrate, the slightly bizarre concrete construction put up by the Emperor Khai Dinh, who ruled from 1916 to 1925, but who spent a good deal of time enjoying himself in France. This is reflected in the main hall of his mortuary complex, which looks surprisingly like a casino from Nice or Monte Carlo. But this strange exterior is as nothing to the surprise within. You enter in darkness, someone trips a switch and suddenly, under arc lights, you see the larger-than-life gilded bronze statue of Khai Dinh himself, seated on his throne, sternly gazing over the hills to some distant point – perhaps a favourite restaurant in Cannes!

In Hué itself I was able to combine culture and food as it was only a short cyclo ride from the Purple Forbidden City along the river bank to the main market, one of the largest in the country. The evident abundance of all the regular Southeast Asian produce was a sign that the country is undergoing a rebirth of private enterprise, with stalls selling ducks and pigs. These were once rarities but are now seen everywhere, and I was told that demand for such delicacies is insatiable. That and the number of shaky trucks pounding along the main roads, exacerbating the already hair-raising traffic, are the best testimony to the restoration of the private distribution system.

There are two other aspects of a Vietnamese market that stand out: first the extraordinarily large snails that you see in buckets and heaps everywhere. I never found them on any menu, though I was told they are a popular staple, stuffed and cooked with pork and herbs. Being about the size of tennis balls, they were clearly a useful foodstuff. I was, however, less happy about the other notable product on sale in Hué and elsewhere – dog. I can eat most things, but being a dog-lover this is too much for me. I had seen dogs in China, in Canton, but they had been alive in cages, waiting for a buyer – bad enough, but nothing compared to the area in most Vietnamese markets where you find a butcher's slab with dog's heads, dog steaks and, yes, dog sausages! I turned and fled, but it gave me bad dreams.

Fortunately my hotel had an excellent restaurant, the Riverside Café, which specialized in classic Vietnamese cookery as well as local delicacies like deep-fried quail, steamed fish with vegetables, and crab claws wrapped in prawn and shrimp, several of which I have included here. Overall, Hué was my best experience for fine food. This was undoubtedly due to a phenomenon I'd witnessed in China, where the new Western-built hotels have brought in top chefs from Hong Kong and Singapore who are beginning to revive the forgotten glories of Chinese cuisine in its native land. For similar reasons the An Phu restaurant, not far from the hotel at 14b Chu Van An, was worth a visit because it too is locked into the tourist trade and has raised standards that are elsewhere abysmally low. One hears much about the destructive effects of global tourism, but in terms of food and restaurants the effects are often highly beneficial in places where the old traditions have nearly died out.

**Farmers carrying
straw near Song Can**

I did find one hardy survivor – a little food stall near the point where the Perfume River branches off into the Nhug River, forming a small lake where fishermen bang the sides of their boats to drive the shoals of freshwater fish into nets stretched on poles across the water. Drawn to the sound of this drumming, I saw a small shop-house on the river bank, where a woman was squatting at a charcoal brazier, patiently making complicated pancakes. These turned out to be the most delicious things I ate during my entire visit – a crispy rice flour base filled with pork, shrimp and beansprouts with a touch of egg, served with a dipping sauce heavily flavoured with mint. The surroundings were less than salubrious. Stacked tins of motor oil suggested that the primary function of the business was car maintenance, though I've eaten in worse places and it hardly detracted from the pleasure of watching the deft way in which the woman produced these delicate morsels.

Feeling a lot better about Vietnam, I headed for the coast and the pleasant drive over the mountains to the port of Danang. This had been at the centre of American military activity, famous as a 'rest and recreation centre' where GIs relaxed before returning to the front line. Having suffered terribly at the hands of rioting South Vietnamese troops, followed by vengeful North Vietnamese occupiers, the city is now struggling to recapture some of its former zest. Superbly situated on a promontory where the Han River flows into the Bay of Danang and thence on to the South China Sea, the port is already bustling with ocean-going vessels as business revives. So much so that there was no room in the Marco Polo, the best hotel in town, which set me on a long and increasingly frantic search for a decent place to stay. Eventually I discovered a brand new block and found myself inside the just-opened, and hopefully named, Modern Hotel where the owners' enthusiasm made up for what they lacked in experience. Better

still, the hotel was right on Bach Dang Street, which runs along the river beside the main port area, near to most of the town's sights and activities.

It was only a short walk to the Cho Han market, a rather gloomy covered arcade that spills out into the surrounding streets and which gave me an even wider view of what Vietnam has to offer. Happily, the Cho Han is a vegetable market, so there was no dog stall in evidence, but what struck me most were the little shops in the surrounding streets that specialize in cooking equipment, most of it locally made. Here it is clear that, despite the surface crudeness – hand-forged scissors, heavy knives and axes, charcoal stoves cannibalized from old tins – Vietnam has managed to develop a simple technological base. There was also evidence of a considerable amount of canning, bottling and packaging of preserved and dried ingredients, from the well-known nuoc nam fish sauce that is exported world wide, down to neat little packets of spices with brightly coloured pop-art graphics, a treasure trove for collectors of naive art.

The most telling sign of economic growth is Danang's rush-hour scramble, with countless bicycles pouring down every road. When this coincides with the end of the school day, you are treated to the extraordinary spectacle of hundreds of pretty Vietnamese girls riding home, all wearing the traditional au dai, the long white jacket split at the sides that manages to be simultaneously modest and revealing, and which is usually topped off with a traditional white shell hat. Some individualistic souls try to vary this with a woolly pom-pom hat or a straw bonnet with artificial flowers, but whatever they wear, everyone smiles.

After bicycling girls, the next best thing in Danang is the Cham Museum. Originally set up by the French, this houses the stunning collection of sculpture found on local excavations, much of it heavily influenced by Indian originals with statues of Shiva, Brahma and Vishnu. That aside, little of the French era has survived. The only person who tried to speak the language to me was the old guardian of the Catholic Cathedral, who was touchingly eager for me to admire the stained glass windows and plaster saints, all of which had been 'Made in France'.

Memories of the American era are evoked by a trip to the once-famous China Beach, subject of many pop songs, where the GIs used to relax between missions. On the way out of town I noticed a building surrounded by wooden frames, on which strands of yellow egg noodles were drying. Stopping the taxi, I went in to find a real old-fashioned noodle factory, where a huge stone wheel was squeezing the dough before it passed through a second machine that separated it into long strands. I did not, however, see any eggs, confirming what I had long suspected, that most egg noodle in Asia is made with artificial colouring – good news for vegetarians, if nothing else! Indeed, any vegetarians are well covered in Danang as there are several purely vegetarian eating places around the Cho Han market, though they follow the

**An old lady about
to enjoy her meal**

Rush hour, Danang

Chinese practice of serving up non-meat meals dressed to look like meat – beancurd rabbits or chickens made out of mushrooms – so you don't feel you're missing anything.

My last full day in Vietnam was the high spot of the visit: a drive out to the coastal town of Hoi An, an old Chinese trading post that is surely one of the prettiest places in Asia. It was to Hoi An that the Chinese junks came, from the seventeenth century onwards, joined later by sailors from Holland, Portugal and Japan. After crossing the pretty little 'Japanese Covered Bridge', the visitor can stroll down a delightful main street, past handsome teakwood merchants houses and the sumptuously decorated temples and pagodas that were built by the various sailors' guilds, whose members endowed them with sculptures and furnishings brought from a homeland that many of them would never see again. Best of all are the houses themselves, some of them dating back to the eighteenth century, whose dark salons are furnished with lacquered tables and chairs inlaid with mother-of-pearl, the walls hung with long-robed ancestor paintings under glass, silk hangings and tall vases decorated with wispy reeds and wading herons. Each salon leads out into a brightly lit courtyard, then on to another set of rooms, ending in a kitchen, beyond which is a tiny walled garden. It is a vision of an ideal Chinese home, born of nostalgia and almost impossible to find in China itself.

In a tangible way, Hoi An sets Vietnamese history in context, revealing its 'other', Chinese side, the element that makes it subtly different from its neighbours in Southeast Asia. The kitchens in these Sino-Vietnamese mansions are living museums of the country's culinary history. In the rest of the region, cooking takes place at ground level on a charcoal burner, but in Hoi An you find

a high, waist-level brick platform with two openings, one for a wok, the other for a steamer, under which are the fires. There is a side table for preparation, and outside in the yard stand large earthenware water jars. The room itself is blackened and scented with the age-old aromas of cooking.

Back in Danang that night I was again treated to one of those sudden swings between heaven and hell that seems to characterize a country in transition – I managed to find a restaurant that had no food to sell, none at all! The Modern Hotel did manage to save the day by coming up with a Vietnamese clay pot of meat and vegetables, even if the plastic spoon was starting to melt in the hot stock! The return journey the following day also brought out some of the things that still make Vietnam difficult for visitors: the long wait for a connection at Hanoi airport, with nothing to eat except sticky approximations of French pâtisserie, followed by endless queues past officials who clearly hadn't learned how to work their computer terminals, though at least my worries about having the wrong documents proved groundless.

Overall it had been a fascinating trip, though I would advise anyone who wants to see the country to take an organized tour; the individual traveller is forced to waste a good deal of time just arranging quite simple things. South Vietnam has already established international standard hotels with first-class food and, if things go on as they are, the rest of the country should follow. For the present, a visit is still something of an adventure, but with Hué and Hoi An in mind, one that is well worth the effort.

BANH KHOAI
VIETNAMESE SAVOURY PANCAKE

INGREDIENTS
- 115g (4oz) rice flour
- 1 teaspoon ground turmeric
- ½ teaspoon salt
- 3 tablespoons oil
- 2 garlic cloves, finely chopped
- 60g (2oz) minced pork
- 60g (2oz) pork fillet, thinly sliced
- 60g (2oz) small shrimps
- 60g (2oz) beansprouts
- 60g (2oz) onion, finely chopped
- 1 teaspoon sugar
- 1 tablespoon fish sauce
- ¼ teaspoon ground white pepper
- 1 egg

FOR THE SAUCE:
- 60g (2oz) cucumber, chopped into small dice
- 60g (2oz) carrot, chopped into small dice
- 60g (2oz) onion, chopped into small dice
- 2 large fresh red or green chillies, finely chopped
- 20 mint leaves, coarsely chopped
- 2 tablespoons fish sauce
- 1 teaspoon sugar
- 2 tablespoons rice vinegar or white wine vinegar

This was the pancake I watched being made in Hué and it was probably the tastiest thing I ate in Vietnam.

PREPARATION

First make the sauce: mix all the ingredients together and set aside.

In a bowl, mix the flour, turmeric and salt with 450ml (¾ pint) water to make a smooth batter. Set aside.

Heat 2 tablespoons of the oil in a wok or deep frying pan and stir-fry all the remaining ingredients except the egg in succession, stirring after each addition. Check that the pork slices are just cooked through, then remove from the heat and set aside.

Break the egg into a bowl, beat it lightly and set aside.

Place a flat-bottomed 20cm (8in) crêpe or omelette pan on a high heat. Pour in a little oil (no more than 1 tablespoon), spread it evenly with a spatula and pour off any excess. Stir the batter, then pour in just enough to coat the bottom of the pan.

Using a spatula to check when the underside of this pancake is almost cooked, place a little mound of the stir-fried ingredients on one half of the pancake, just off centre. Drip about 1 tablespoon of the beaten egg over this, then lift the opposite corner of the pancake over the filled half. Press down lightly, leave to cook briefly, then lift out of the pan and serve at once. Repeat the procedure until all the batter and/or the stuffing is used up.

Serve the pancakes with the sauce.

BO XAO MANG
BEEF WITH BAMBOO SHOOTS

INGREDIENTS
- 2 tablespoons sesame oil
- 225g (8oz) beef steak, thinly sliced
- 115g (4oz) bamboo shoots, thinly sliced
- 1 tablespoon fish sauce
- ½ teaspoon sugar
- 1 large fresh red chilli, finely chopped
- 2 spring onions, chopped into 2.5cm (1in) lengths
- 1 teaspoon white sesame seeds

PREPARATION

Heat the oil and briefly stir-fry the beef until just cooked through.

Add all the remaining ingredients in turn, stirring between each addition.

As soon as the sesame seeds are stirred in, remove from the heat, turn out on a plate and serve.

MI XAO DA NANG

DANANG FRIED NOODLE

INGREDIENTS

- 2 tablespoons oil
- 60g (2oz) onions, coarsely chopped
- 115g (4oz) beef steak, thinly sliced
- 115g (4oz) egg noodles, soaked if dried
- 60g (2oz) black fungus mushroom, coarsely chopped (see page 19)
- 60g (2oz) celery, coarsely chopped
- 60g (2oz) tomatoes, coarsely chopped
- 1 tablespoon fish sauce
- 1 tablespoon light soy sauce
- 1 tablespoon sugar
- ¼ teaspoon ground white pepper
- Coriander leaves to garnish

This is a dish prepared with the yellow noodles I saw being made on the road to China Beach outside Danang. I've suggested using beef here; but, as with most noodle dishes, you could substitute pork, chicken, seafood, or even a firm vegetable like mushrooms or broccoli, as required.

PREPARATION

Heat the oil in a wok or deep frying pan and fry the onions briefly. Add the beef and stir-fry until almost cooked through.

Add all the remaining ingredients except the coriander in succession, stirring between each addition.

As soon as the ground pepper is stirred in, turn the mixture out on a plate, garnish with the coriander and serve.

PHO GA HANH XAO

CHICKEN NOODLE SOUP WITH CRISPY SHALLOTS

INGREDIENTS

- 2 tablespoons oil
- 2 small red shallots, finely chopped
- 450ml (¾ pint) chicken stock (see page 14)
- 60g (2oz) beansprouts
- 115g (4oz) medium flat rice flour noodles (see page 11), soaked if dried
- 85g (3oz) boneless chicken, thinly sliced
- 1 tablespoon fish sauce
- 1 tablespoon light soy sauce
- ½ teaspoon sugar
- 1 spring onion, finely chopped

This is the classic Vietnamese noodle dish in which the use of shallot and fish sauce clearly show how different the country's cuisine is from that of China. It is a wonderfully comforting dish for a wet or cold day.

PREPARATION

Heat the oil in a wok and fry the shallots until golden brown. Remove from the heat and reserve both the oil and the shallots together.

Heat the stock in a pan and simmer until required.

Bring a pan of water to the boil. Using a mesh ladle strainer, dip the beansprouts in the water to blanch them for 10 seconds. Remove, shake to drain well and place in a large serving bowl. Repeat the process with the noodles, blanching them for 20 seconds, then the chicken, again for 20 seconds.

Add the fish and soy sauces to the bowl with the sugar. Stir well. Pour the hot stock into the bowl and stir. Sprinkle with the chopped spring onion, then pour over about half of the oil and shallots.

Serve, with the remaining oil and shallots in a side dish for diners to use as required.

BUN THIT HEO NUONG
GRILLED PORK WITH RICE VERMICELLI

INGREDIENTS
- 225g (8oz) pork, thinly sliced

FOR THE MARINADE:
- 1 stalk of lemon grass, finely chopped then pounded
- 2 garlic cloves, finely chopped then pounded
- 5 small red shallots, finely chopped then pounded
- 2 tablespoons fish sauce
- 1 teaspoon sugar
- ½ teaspoon ground white pepper
- 1 tablespoon sesame oil
- 1 teaspoon white sesame seeds

FOR THE SAUCE:
- 2 tablespoons fish sauce
- 1 tablespoon rice vinegar
- 1 teaspoon sugar
- 1 garlic clove, finely chopped
- 2 small fresh red or green chillies, finely chopped

FOR THE NOODLES:
- 115g (4oz) rice vermicelli (see page 11)
- 60g (2oz) beansprouts
- 20 sweet basil leaves

While this can be served as a main course, it also makes a very satisfying one-dish meal.

PREPARATION

In a bowl, mix all the marinade ingredients. Place the sliced pork in the bowl and turn to coat thoroughly. Leave to marinate for 30 minutes.

While the pork is marinating, make the sauce: mix all the ingredients thoroughly with 1 tablespoon water and turn into a serving bowl.

Preheat a moderate grill.

Make the noodles: heat a large pan of water. When boiling, place the vermicelli in a long-handled strainer and plunge into the pan briefly. Remove, drain and turn out on a large serving platter. Arrange the raw beansprouts and sweet basil leaves to one side of the bed of noodles.

Grill the marinated pork until golden brown on both sides: this should only take a minute. Remove, place on a separate dish and serve with the vermicelli and the sauce.

Diners should take some vermicelli and some beansprouts and basil leaves on their plate and pour over a little sauce, then put some grilled pork beside the mixture.

THAN CHAN CHANH
KIDNEYS WITH MINT AND LIME

INGREDIENTS
- 2 pigs' kidneys, thinly sliced to keep the distinct 'comma' outline of the kidney
- 115g (4oz) onion, finely chopped
- 1 tablespoon finely chopped ginger
- 2 tablespoons lime juice
- ¼ teaspoon ground black pepper
- ¼ teaspoon salt
- 20 mint leaves

Many people today are resistant to kidneys because of the strong flavour, which is often disguised by thick sauces. This recipe is remarkable because the Vietnamese love of fresh citrus flavours removes any trace of unpleasantness, resulting in a dish which is surprisingly sharp and fresh.

PREPARATION

Bring a pan of water to the boil. Put in the sliced kidney and blanch for 1 minute. Remove and drain.

Place in a large bowl and add all the other ingredients. Stir well, turn out on a plate and serve.

NEM CUON SONG

FRESH 'NEM' SPRING ROLL

INGREDIENTS

- 115g (4oz) lean pork
- 60g (2oz) rice vermicelli (see page 11)
- 115g (4oz) small shrimps
- 60g (2oz) beansprouts
- 3 tablespoons ground peanuts
- 2 tablespoons coarsely chopped coriander leaves
- 12 sheets of banh trang rice paper (see page 11)

TO SERVE:

- Lettuce leaves
- Mint leaves

FOR THE PHUANG NAM DIPPING SAUCE:

- 2 tablespoons fish sauce
- 2 tablespoons rice vinegar or white wine vinegar
- 1 tablespoon water
- 1 teaspoon very finely chopped ginger
- 1 teaspoon sugar
- 2 small fresh red or green chillies, finely chopped
- 1 garlic clove, finely chopped

PREPARATION

First make the phuang nam dipping sauce: mix all the ingredients together and serve in individual bowls.

Heat a pan of water and boil the pork until just cooked through. Remove, drain well and chop very finely. Set aside.

Change the water and bring to the boil. Using a mesh ladle strainer, dip the rice vermicelli in the boiling water for about 10 seconds. Remove and plunge into cold water to arrest the cooking. Drain, break up roughly and set aside.

Repeat the blanching procedure with the shrimps, for 5 seconds only. Remove, drain, finely chop and set aside. Repeat with the beansprouts, blanching for 10 seconds only.

Give each diner a plate on which is laid a folded napkin that has been soaked in cold water. Next, arrange the blanched ingredients on a serving platter along with the rice paper sheets and mounds of the ground peanuts and coriander leaves. Place this on the table with the dipping bowls and with another serving platter bearing the lettuce and mint leaves.

To make a nem: take a rice paper sheet and dampen it on a wet napkin. Lay it on a plate and arrange a mix of the blanched ingredients in a line. Sprinkle this filling with the peanuts and coriander. Take the near edge of the sheet and roll it over the filling to form a tube: the dampened paper should stick together, making a manageable roll that can be lifted and dipped in the sauce. This should be eaten with the lettuce and mint leaves.

GOI GA

CHICKEN SALAD WITH MINT AND NUTS

INGREDIENTS

- 175g (6oz) skinless chicken breast fillet
- 85g (3oz) beansprouts
- 85g (3oz) cucumber, cut in half lengthways, deseeded, then cut into fine matchsticks about 5cm (2in) long
- 85g (3oz) onion, finely chopped
- 2 tablespoons fish sauce
- 2 tablespoons lime juice
- 1 tablespoon finely chopped mint leaves
- 2 tablespoons ground roasted peanuts
- 2 teaspoons sesame seeds, dry-fried

This mix of crisp salad heavily flavoured with mint seems to me to be more typical of true Vietnamese cuisine than the meat in thick sauces often served in Vietnamese restaurants in the West.

PREPARATION

Bring a pan of water to the boil, add the chicken breast and simmer until cooked through. Remove and allow to cool.

Shred the meat into small pieces over a bowl, allowing any liquid it may still retain to fall into the bowl. Put all the remaining ingredients into the bowl and stir well. Turn out on a plate and serve.

CANG CUA CHIEN

DEEP-FRIED CRAB CLAWS IN A PORK AND PRAWN ENVELOPE

INGREDIENTS

- 85g (3oz) minced pork
- 115g (4oz) shelled and deveined raw prawns, finely chopped
- 1 egg
- 1 garlic clove, finely chopped
- 1 tablespoon fish sauce
- 1 tablespoon oyster sauce
- 1 teaspoon cornflour
- ¼ teaspoon ground white pepper
- 6–8 crab claws (depending on size)
- Oil for deep-frying

FOR THE PLUM SAUCE:

- 1 whole preserved plum (see page 19)
- 225ml (8fl oz) rice vinegar or white wine vinegar
- 5 tablespoons sugar

I liked this so much when I tried it at Hué's Riverside Café, not only for its rich mix of flavours but also because it looks so good. It makes a dramatic dinner-party offering.

PREPARATION

First make the plum sauce: with a fork, shred the flesh of the plum from its stone – this should leave you with tiny scrapings. Set aside. Place the vinegar and sugar in a saucepan and heat to make a syrup. Stir in the plum scrapings, turn into a dipping dish and set aside.

In a bowl, thoroughly mix all the remaining ingredients except the crab claws and oil. Divide the mixture by the number of crab claws (6–8) and mould a piece round the meaty section at the end of each claw, leaving the pincer itself exposed.

Preheat the oil and deep-fry the coated crab claws until the moulded envelopes are a deep golden brown. Remove, drain and serve with the plum sauce.

CHA GIO CHAY

VEGETARIAN FRIED SPRING ROLL

INGREDIENTS

- 115g (4oz) cellophane noodles, soaked (see page 11)
- 30g (1oz) black fungus mushroom, finely chopped (see page 19)
- 60g (2oz) carrot, grated
- 60g (2oz) white cabbage, grated
- 1 tablespoon light soy sauce
- 1 garlic clove, finely chopped
- 1 tablespoon ground roasted peanuts
- ¼ teaspoon ground white pepper
- 1 teaspoon sugar
- 15 sheets of banh trang rice paper (see page 11)
- Oil for deep-frying

TO SERVE:

- Phuang nam dipping sauce (page 122)
- Lettuce leaves
- Mint leaves

PREPARATION

Drain the noodles, coarsely chop and place in a bowl. Add all the vegetables, soy sauce, garlic, peanuts, pepper and sugar. Mix well.

Fill a flat soup bowl with hot water and drag each rice paper sheet through it to soften. Lay the damp sheets on a board and place a line of the noodle mixture across each. Take up an edge parallel to the line and roll the sheet into a tube. When you reach the centre tuck in a little of the outside edges then continue rolling until the tube is complete – the dampened paper should stick together. There will be approximately 60 spring rolls.

When all the rolls are complete, heat the oil and deep-fry the rolls in batches of 3–4, until golden brown. Remove, drain and keep warm, uncovered, until all are done.

Cut each roll into 4 pieces, then serve with the phuang nam dipping sauce and lettuce and mint leaves.

CA HAP NAM
STEAMED FISH WITH MUSHROOMS

INGREDIENTS

- I whole small sea bass (or similar firm fish)
- 2 garlic cloves, thinly sliced
- 60g (2oz) button mushrooms, thinly sliced
- 60g (2oz) black fungus mushroom, soaked, drained then thinly sliced (see page 19)
- 60g (2oz) carrots, finely chopped
- 60g (2oz) onion, finely chopped
- 2 tablespoons light soy sauce
- ½ teaspoon sugar
- ¼ teaspoon ground white pepper
- A grating of nutmeg

This is my version of the steamed fish with vegetables that I ate at the Riverside Café in Hué. I've simplified the number of vegetables, making it mainly a mushroom dish. You could add more.

PREPARATION

Place the sea bass on an oval plate that will fit into the upper compartment of a steamer. Place all the remaining ingredients on top of the fish, spreading them evenly. Place the dish in the steamer and cook until the fish is just cooked through, about 15 minutes, depending on size. Remove from the steamer, dab away any water from the dish with kitchen paper, then serve.

CHIM CUOC CHIEN
DEEP-FRIED QUAIL

INGREDIENTS

- I teaspoon coriander seeds
- 3 garlic cloves
- ½ teaspoon black peppercorns
- I stalk of lemon grass, coarsely chopped
- 4 quails
- 2 tablespoons light soy sauce
- 2 teaspoons honey
- Oil for deep-frying
- Lime Dip (see page 129), to serve

PREPARATION

In a mortar, pound the coriander seeds, garlic cloves, peppercorns and lemon grass to make a paste. Spread this over the quails, then sprinkle the birds with soy sauce. Spoon over the honey and leave to marinate for 1 hour. When ready to cook, heat the oil for deep-frying and cook the quail until golden brown (you could also barbecue them). Serve with the lime dip.

NOM DU DU THIT BO NUONG
GRILLED BEEF WITH RAW PAPAYA

INGREDIENTS

- 115g (4oz) lean beef steak
- 85g (3oz) green raw papaya, grated or slivered
- 60g (2oz) carrot, grated or slivered, as above
- 4 small fresh red or green chillies, finely chopped
- I tablespoon fish sauce
- I tablespoon lime juice
- ½ teaspoon sugar
- I tablespoon ground roasted peanuts
- 10 mint leaves

This dish seemed to be especially popular in the port of Danang, to judge by the number of food sellers cooking it on portable stoves. It is one of those dishes that the diner can adjust to taste by adding more fish sauce and lime juice as required. I've given a minimum amount here, but you could put out little bowls of these flavours for diners to take if they wish.

PREPARATION

Grill the steak to taste, then thinly slice it and place in a serving bowl. Add all the other ingredients and mix thoroughly. Turn out on a dish and serve.

TOM HAP MIEN DONG
PRAWN AND VERMICELLI HOT-POT

INGREDIENTS

- 85g (3oz) cellophane noodles (see page 11)
- 60g (2oz) black fungus mushroom
- 2 spring onions, cut into 2.5cm (1in) lengths
- 1 tablespoon finely chopped ginger
- 1 tablespoon oyster sauce
- 1 tablespoon light soy sauce
- ½ teaspoon sugar
- 175g (6oz) shelled raw prawns
- A grinding of black pepper

For this dish you will need a clay pot with a lid or at least a heavy-based saucepan, otherwise the noodles may stick to the pan and burn. Don't leave a plastic spoon in the pot!!!

PREPARATION

Place the ingredients in turn in layers in the clay pot: noodles on the bottom, the prawns on top. Cover, place on a moderate heat and cook for 5 minutes. Check that the prawns have changed colour and are opaque and cooked through. Remove from the heat and serve from the pot.

BO CAU ROTI
GRILLED PIGEON

INGREDIENTS

- 2 pigeons
- 4 tablespoons sesame oil
- 1 stalk of lemon grass, finely chopped
- 2 tablespoons oyster sauce
- 1 teaspoon sugar
- 5 small fresh red chillies, finely chopped
- a sprinkling of salt

PREPARATION

Cut the pigeons in half lengthways and set aside. Briefly pound the lemon grass.

In a bowl, mix all the remaining ingredients thoroughly, then coat the pigeon halves with the mixture and leave to marinate for 1 hour.

Preheat a moderate grill and grill the pigeons until both sides are golden and no liquid appears when the breast is pierced with a skewer.

Cut the birds in half lengthways to serve.

DAU PHU XAO RAU
BEANCURD WITH STIR-FRIED MIXED VEGETABLES

INGREDIENTS

- 2 trays white soft beancurd, 7.5cm (3in) square
- Oil for deep-frying
- ½ teaspoon cornflour
- 2 tablespoons oil
- 2 garlic cloves, finely chopped
- 1 teaspoon finely chopped ginger
- 60g (2oz) bamboo shoots, thinly sliced
- 60g (2oz) carrots, thinly sliced
- 60g (2oz) beansprouts
- 60g (2oz) spring onions
- 1 teaspoon black bean sauce
- 2 tablespoons light soy sauce
- ½ teaspoon sugar

PREPARATION

Cut the 2 beancurd blocks into smaller cubes about 2.5cm (1in) square. Preheat the oil for deep-frying and fry the cubes until yellow (not brown). Remove, drain and set aside. Cut the spring onions into 2.5cm (1in) lengths.

Mix the cornflour with 2 tablespoons water and set aside.

In a wok or deep frying pan, heat the 2 tablespoons oil and fry the garlic until golden. Then add all the other ingredients in turn, stirring between each addition.

Stir in just enough of the cornflour mixture to thicken the dish slightly.

Turn out on a plate, place the fried beancurd cubes on top and serve.

CHE DAU XANH

MOONG BEANS IN DARK SUGAR

INGREDIENTS
- 225g (8oz) moong beans
- 175g (6oz) dark sugar

This recipe is simplicity itself, but the result is surprisingly tasty and makes the perfect end to a dinner party. Moong beans keep well in a tightly sealed jar, especially if stored in a refrigerator, so this is a useful, easy-to-make stand-by.

PREPARATION

Dry-fry the moong beans until they begin to give off a pleasing aroma.

Transfer to a saucepan and cover with 1 litre (1¾ pints) water. Bring to the boil and simmer for 5 minutes. Remove from the heat and drain away the discoloured water.

Return the beans to the pan and cover with a similar quantity of water. Bring to the boil and simmer for 5 minutes.

Add the sugar and bring back to the boil, stirring well. Check that the beans are soft (if not, cook for a few minutes longer).

Remove from the heat and serve hot or chilled from the refrigerator.

SA SUON CHIEN

DEEP-FRIED SPARE RIBS WITH CHILLI AND LEMON GRASS

INGREDIENTS
- 450g (1lb) young pork spare ribs
- 2 tablespoons sesame oil
- 2 garlic cloves, finely chopped and briefly pounded
- 1 stalk of lemon grass, finely chopped and briefly pounded
- 4 small fresh red chillies, finely chopped and briefly pounded
- ½ teaspoon salt
- 1 teaspoon sugar
- ½ teaspoon ground white pepper
- 2 tablespoons fish sauce
- Oil for deep-frying

FOR THE LIME DIP:
- 1 teaspoon salt
- 1 teaspoon ground white pepper
- 3 tablespoons lime juice

I found this, unexpectedly, in a noodle shop in Hanoi. It's very spicy and makes a good sharp appetizer to serve with drinks. The lime dip is the same as Cambodian Tik Marij (see page 91).

PREPARATION

If the spare ribs are bought in a large piece, separate them and chop each rib into 5cm (2in) pieces. Set aside.

In a large bowl, mix all the remaining ingredients except the oil for deep-frying. Add the spare rib pieces, mix thoroughly and leave to marinate for at least 1 hour.

Preheat the oil and deep-fry the spare ribs in batches until golden brown. Remove from the oil, drain and keep warm until all are done.

While the spare ribs are frying, make the lime dip: mix all the ingredients together and serve in a dipping bowl.

Place the fried spare ribs on a dish and serve with the dip.

BANH CHUOI
BANANA AND SWEET POTATO FRITTERS

INGREDIENTS

- 115g (4oz) rice flour
- 225ml (8fl oz) coconut milk
- ½ teaspoon salt
- 60g (2oz) sugar
- 5 small or 2 large unripe bananas (the skins just turning yellow)
- 1 medium sweet potato
- Oil for deep-frying

This is the delicacy that the street vendor was making near my hotel in Hanoi and was the first thing I ate in Vietnam. Banana fritters are sold all over Southeast Asia, but this combination with sweet potato is especially good. The street seller in Hanoi had a neat way of frying this while measuring out a portion for sale – she used a flat 'shovel' spatula on which she arranged 2 slices of banana, then in the opposite direction, 2 slices of sweet potato. She dipped the loaded shovel into the hot oil, lifted it out and slipped the golden fritters into a twist of paper.

PREPARATION

Mix the flour, coconut milk, salt and sugar to a smooth mixture and set aside. Cut the small bananas in half or the long bananas into 3 pieces each. This should give pieces about 7.5cm (3in) long. Cut these pieces lengthways into strips about 1cm (½in) thick. Do the same thing with the sweet potato: cut it in half, then cut the halves into thin strips.

Preheat the oil for deep-frying. Dip the strips in the batter, shake off any excess and place them in the hot oil. Fry until golden brown, remove, drain and serve immediately.

CHA CA NAM
GRILLED FISH WITH MUSHROOM SAUCE

INGREDIENTS

- 4 tablespoons sesame oil
- 1 small whole firm-fleshed fish (such as trout)
- 5 small red shallots, coarsely chopped
- 115g (4oz) dried Chinese mushrooms, soaked, drained then thinly sliced (see page 19)
- 1 tablespoon fish sauce
- 1 tablespoon light soy sauce
- ½ teaspoon cornflour
- 3 spring onions, cut into 2.5cm (1in) lengths
- ¼ teaspoon ground white pepper

PREPARATION

Pour 2 tablespoons of the sesame oil over the fish, coat well and leave for 15 minutes. Preheat a moderate grill. In the meantime, heat the remaining oil and fry the shallots until crispy and golden. Remove and set aside, retaining the oil. Grill the fish until just cooked through. Using your fingers, break up the fish into chunks, carefully removing any bones. Place the fish pieces on a serving dish and set aside. Reheat the reserved oil and stir-fry the mushrooms briefly. Add the fish sauce and the light soy sauce and stir. Mix the cornflour with 3 tablespoons water and add just enough of this mixture to thicken the liquid in the pan slightly. Add the spring onions and the ground white pepper and stir once. Remove from the heat and pour over the fish. Scatter the crispy fried shallots on top and serve.

Burma

BE NICE TO NATS

On my first night in Burma I was invited to eat with some friends at their home in Golden Valley Road, in the garden suburb just beyond the main commercial centre of the city the British called Rangoon, but which to its inhabitants has always been Yangon. Many things about that evening revealed aspects of the current situation in the country. Burma is supposed to have undergone a prolonged revolutionary experience, shut off from the outside world, yet here was an old, well-placed family in Western clothes, giving a dinner party in the sort of smart detached house with front porch and bay windows that you might find in a quiet English suburb. There were comfortable armchairs and servants in the traditional wrap-around longyis, offering whisky and soda or gin and tonic before the meal. Somehow this family of professional people – diplomats, doctors and teachers, with a sprinkling of businessmen and women – had survived the upheavals since the country's independence in 1948 and the subsequent years of military rule, keeping their way of life reasonably intact.

That night there was talk of the future, of hopes that Burma would rejoin the outside world at last, that the economy would improve and democracy flourish. Of course there were fears, too. Only a short walk away was the compound where Aung San Suu Kyi was living under house-arrest since her victory in the national elections that were annulled by the grimly named SLORC (the State Law and Restoration Council). This was 1995 and since then Aung San Suu Kyi has called for a tourist boycott. Some opposition leaders do not agree with her and wish the country to remain open to visitors, so individual travellers will have to decide for themselves. In a sense this means that little has changed. For much of the period since the British handed over power, tourism was discouraged and only 24-hour visas were issued. An extension to seven days didn't alter much, as it was still impossible to see the country's main historical sites in so limited a time. This was why so many Thais, myself included, had never visited one of our closest neighbours. It was the recent decision to grant full visas that encouraged me to fly on to Rangoon after my visit to Vietnam, a swing to the opposite pole of Southeast Asia's cultural pendulum – from France and China to Britain and India.

In Rangoon it is the Britishness you see first – the imposing Imperial buildings, with their mix of Classical and Gothic, the aston-

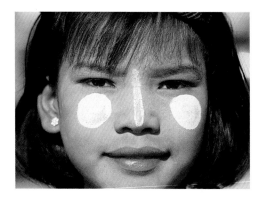

Protection from the sun with a powder made from Thanaka bark

ishing number of parks, gardens and flower beds that are the great legacy of the British municipal tradition. Even my hotel was set in its own grounds and, although now called Best Executive Suites, was once a set of bungalows used by young unmarried officers out from Britain to administer this distant colonial outpost. Each bungalow still has its own servant, who potters around, mothering her charges, cooking a full English breakfast of bacon and eggs with toast and marmalade, served· under the cooling draught of the revolving ceiling fans.

The British chose to call the country Burma, though historically this has always been its informal name, the formal title being Myanmar – rather like The Netherlands (formal) and Holland (informal). SLORC has proposed reversing the British choice by calling the country Myanmar and using more local versions of place names such as Yangon for Rangoon, but until this is confirmed by a properly elected government the outside world will no doubt wish to apply a policy of 'wait-and-see'.

The word Burma is derived from the Bamars, the country's largest ethnic group, who occupy the central area along the River Irrawaddy, from Rangoon up to Pagan and on to the old capital of Mandalay. While this is all most visitors can hope to see, it is as well to bear in mind that there are some 67 ethnic groups that make up Burma's extraordinarily diverse population. These include the Paduang 'Giraffe Women', their necks stretched by up to 25cm (10in) by the copper and brass necklaces that tribal tradition expects them to wear. There are also some groups, like the Shan and the Karen, still fighting for independence from what they see as Bamar dominance.

Apart from the change of names, one of the main effects of British rule was to bring the country closer to its Western neighbour – for a time it was absorbed into the Indian Empire. Even when Burma was separately run, the colonial power continued to import Indian soldiers, administrators and traders. You get a glimpse of this era of the Raj behind the neo-classical façade of Rangoon's Strand Hotel. Despite being recently upgraded to 'international' standard, this still retains much of its old-world charm, with Indian waiters pottering about, serving afternoon tea in shuttered rooms to white-suited figures slumped in club chairs.

Even the city's main emporium, the old Scott Market – now the Bogyoke Aung San Market – a series of cavernous halls, has the air of an Indian bazaar. There are black-market moneychangers and rows of cloth-merchants' stalls stacked high with the wonderful, brightly printed longyis that men and women prefer to wear – at least in the evening when relaxing. There are also signs that this Indian link is not the whole story, that rather like the Chinese aspects of Vietnamese life it was more a result of colonialism than something truly at the heart of the nation's culture. After all, the dominant feature of Rangoon's skyline is the great gilded stupa of the fabulous Shwedagon Pagoda, surrounded by a cluster of prayer halls with their massive statues of the Buddha, guarded by giants and mythical creatures. Everything there, from the richly carved and burnished architecture, to the hosts of saffron-robed monks, is so clearly part of the same heritage that you find in Thailand, Laos and Cambodia.

This sense of another tradition is reinforced by the food section of the market, where one is immediately back in the Southeast Asian world of lemon grass and holy basil, of the pungent aromas of fermented fish and purple shrimp paste and, of course, noodle stalls. At one of these I had to try the only Burmese dish that is known outside its borders – what we Thais call kow soy, but which is known in its homeland as Khauk-swe (see page 153). This is a fiery mix of coriander seeds, turmeric, ginger, chilli and shallots, made palatable with coconut milk and soothing egg noodles, a dish that embodies all those various elements, Indian and Southeast Asian, that I had been so aware of since I arrived.

In the past, much of the public restaurant trade was in the hands of Indian or Chinese business-people and every book I have ever read on Burmese food has made it absolutely clear that it can only be found in Burmese homes. Even today, there are hardly any Burmese restaurants outside the country and those few are likely to be run by Indians who left Burma in the difficult years, just as

Temple courtyard in Pagan

Shinpyu ceremony, Mandalay

Vietnamese restaurants abroad are often run by Vietnamese-Chinese exiles. I was therefore eager to see what we would be eating at that dinner on my first evening in Rangoon.

Visually at least, the groaning table seemed to emphasize the Indian connection, with curry dishes surrounded by accompanying vegetables in spicy sauces, and smaller dishes of pickles or hot dips nearby. The aromas, too, leant heavily towards what some authorities on Burmese food call the 'curry seeds' – cumin, coriander, mustard, etc. However, as soon as the rice was served and we got down to some serious eating, it was clear that the cook had used the green saplings and shoots of these seeds as often as the seeds themselves, giving the dishes that lightness and freshness which is part of our regional tradition. There was a prawn curry flavoured with ground turmeric, which was far lighter than the usual heavily sauced Indian curries and closer to the aromatic liquid dishes found in Thailand.

On reflection it could hardly be otherwise, given the history of invasion and counter-invasion that we share. Our Buddhist faith, our art and architecture, our traditional theatre and courtly dances, all have common roots, as does our food. Burmese dishes can be found integrated into the food of Northern Thailand, where there are restaurants that specialize in kow soy noodles, while various incursions into Burma by the Mons are thought to have brought traces of Cambodian cuisine.

I had tracked down some of this history that afternoon in Rangoon when I found a charming antiquarian book shop among the jumble of untouched apartment blocks that give the city its air of decaying Englishness. The shop was tiny and piled high with wonderful treasures: from superb architectural drawings of the country's main temples to old sepia postcards of turn-of-the-century Mandalay and, best of all for me, some locally produced cookbooks printed on cheap rough paper but full of useful recipes and tips. I found one published before the Second World War, in which the names of local ingredients were given in Hindi and the recipes were set amongst advertisements for ghee, the Indian cooking fat. By contrast, a book produced after Independence seemed far less Indian-orientated, while its descriptions of smoky wood-burning stoves – the author recommended a shower after cooking a Burmese meal – gave an authenticity the earlier work

lacked. Of course, some of the attitudes reveal a world far removed from contemporary Western sentiments. While the writer proudly states that 30 per cent of the country's doctors, 40 per cent of its teachers and 43 per cent of its trained economists are women, her advice on how these career-women should handle a dinner party seems almost comic:

'For the best dinners nothing should run on invisible or silent wheels. The more flurry and run for extra cutlery and food the greater the compliment to your guests. Another compliment is if you and your daughters do not eat with them. So seat their men, women, girls and boys with your husband for company, and keep yourself from the distraction of eating your own food in company whose immediate comfort is your responsibility. Instead, after cooking, all have a bath, dress up, eat; then during dinner walk around the table continuously. Audibly urge servants, daughters or enlisted help to refill plates wastefully, to fan the guests if they perspire, and to wave off flies if it is fly season.'

I have to say there was none of this at our dinner party on my first night. My friend is a businesswoman who is trying to set up hotels and restaurants ready for when the country is able to get its tourist industry off the ground, and not someone likely to waste time fanning her guests! Looking at the dishes laid before us, I couldn't resist asking if this was 'real' Burmese food, which provoked some laughter. 'We Burmese eat whatever's good,' was one answer. 'If we eat out, we like to mix things – an Indian curry, a Chinese stir-fry, some Burmese noodles.' So it was just like Thailand, where my family would choose a Chinese restaurant if they were eating out.

'But at home?' I insisted. Again, there were smiles.

'Here in Rangoon, food is quite mixed even at home, but the way it is cooked is very Burmese. Traditionally there was no refrigeration, no means of storing food safely, so everything was caught or bought and certainly cooked the same day, and even in a modern home with a refrigerator that is still the practice. Every morning, early, someone goes to market – it's a great meeting place and a chance to eat something different off one of the food stalls. On top of that, the cooking itself is very fast. Most Burmese kitchen equipment is simple – little more than a large, deep frying pan and one or two saucepans for making curries and other liquid dishes. You could say that while there are some Indian flavours, they are used in ways much closer to Chinese techniques.'

'So, what is real Burmese food?'

'Ah,' said one wise neighbour. 'Real Burmese food is what the real Burmese eat. This is Rangoon, you'll have to look elsewhere.'

In fact, most of our conversation that night revolved round the trip I was planning, for I was due to leave for Pagan the following day. One thing everyone agreed on was that I would find this quite extraordinary, and undoubtedly one of the great experiences of my life. As I was soon to discover, they were not exaggerating. Nothing you have read or heard about Pagan can prepare you for the reality. Before arriving I had barely considered what it must mean to see that flat plain dotted with a few stunted trees beside the Irrawaddy River, on which more than 2,200 temples, pagodas and other religious buildings still stand. The figures are just too large to take in – as well try to imagine the 13,000 buildings that filled the area when Kublai Khan's army swept down to burn the surrounding city in 1287.

It was only as the minibus drove in from the airport that the sheer scale of the place began to sink in. Towering constructions, like the Ananda Temple with its high spire or the Shwesandaw Pagoda with its white bell-like stupa, sit in isolated splendour on the empty land. Still intact, they seem almost as if they were built yesterday, while all around are countless weather-beaten ruins; some no more than a square block of crumbling bricks, others with the remains of a tower or a columned entrance. Nothing is left of the city that sustained these architectural gems – no homes, law courts, army barracks; they were made of wood and perished in the flames. But the temples, hundreds and hundreds of them, have miraculously survived invasions and earthquakes, the last as recent as 1975, to make this one of the greatest, yet least-known, wonders of the world.

Buffalo hauling teak on the banks of the Irrawaddy

If asked which had impressed me most, Angkor Wat or Pagan, I would hesitate, but in the end the sheer scale and variety of Burma's Holy City must attract the prize. Each temple, each pagoda, is different. Some, like the vast Shwezigon, have a cluster of open pavilions, filled with monks and worshippers, much like any major monastic temple in Asia. Others consist of little more than a solid central core around which run cave-like passages that suddenly open to allow space for a statue of the seated Buddha, some painted bright red, mysterious in the semi-darkness. Yet even there you will find a worshipper, perhaps a solitary woman, seated cross-legged in a corner, come to find a cool shelter from the searing afternoon heat, bringing a basket of refreshments, perhaps some spicy split-pea fritters that she can nibble while she rests. That, above all, is what makes Pagan different from other ancient religious sites, for unlike the temples of the Nile or ancient Rome, Pagan has never quite ceased to be a living religious centre. Even the remotest ruin, with little more than the trunk of a shattered Buddha, still has its little offering of flowers and incense, left by the people who live in the nearby town.

Not that the townspeople's task is easy. By government decree they were turned out of the original Pagan settlement a

few years back, in order to prepare the site for the huge influx of tourists that has long been announced but slow to happen. Unconsulted and with little time to prepare, the entire population was transported to a new settlement closer to the river, though they still come back to make offerings at the countless shrines and some attempt to plant crops, mainly peanuts, in the dry soil around the sacred buildings.

I stayed in the government-run Thiri Pyitsaya Hotel near the new town, an adequate place, though I was glad that my friends had told me other places where I could eat. After a hard morning's temple visiting, it was good to sit outside under a shady tree at the River View Restaurant, where a truly magnificent khauk-swe was served up, quite different from the simple version I had eaten in the Rangoon Market. This time there were bowls both of chicken soup and fish in coconut sauce, while the noodles and other ingredients – chopped shallots, chilli, pickled cabbage and pickled garlic – were served separately, ready to be mixed as one chose. The result was that I ate too much and what ought to have been a light snack before more hard sightseeing turned into a feast.

What keeps even an overfed visitor going are the constant surprises offered by the truly astonishing buildings. Each ruler seems to have gone to extraordinary lengths to outshine his predecessors, building high and wide and adding ever more audacious embellishments, much of it during the 11th and 12th centuries BC. One temple offers the unusual spectacle of pairs of identical Buddhas seated side by side, presumably on the principle that two of anything are better than one.

Some temples take considerable effort before they yield up their treasures. One involved a ride up the wide and fast-flowing Irrawaddy in a large 'tourist' pleasure boat. This was too big for the few passengers who elected to make the half-hour journey, hugging the eerily empty water's edge with only the occasional two-man rowing boat to vary the scene. There followed a rather laborious walk along the sandy river bank, then a climb up a cliff to a hollow tower inside which was an enormous Buddha, so high one had to bend back almost double to see its face. A solitary hermit monk guards the place and he offered me tea and sweet baby bananas in return for the chance to talk to someone. I couldn't help feeling that his wooden shack must seem very spooky at night, when he is alone amongst all these deserted ruins and silent statues. He did, however, have some source of electricity, judging by the winking fairy lights he had draped around his private shrine at the back of the room. He had also tried to cheer the place up by covering every surface with snapshots sent to him by passing visitors when they returned home.

Even so short a trip along the Irrawaddy was magical. There is now a luxury cruiser which will allow visitors to make the journey from Pagan to Mandalay in some style – private cabins, first-class restaurant, swimming pool – though even the old river steamers have a certain allure, provided you carry your own supplies and have plenty of good books to read.

Back on land, and somewhat satiated with temples, I decided to visit the Pagan market. At the entrance was the betel seller,

A Paduang 'Giraffe Woman'

making up his refreshing snack of folded betel leaf with its filling of bitter paste and chopped betel nut, often taken to aid digestion after a good meal. Just inside the market were the rice merchants seated beside their open sacks. There you can examine the different varieties and qualities of the precious grain – red, white, green, yellow and black, subdivided into those with rough or smooth grain and husk and those that are long or short, round or fat. Few beyond the farmers themselves can detect such subtleties – for most of us there is simply white rice or the more healthy brown variety, and the white can generally be divided into long-grain or short-grain types. Even I, a regular eater of rice, can make do with that. However, for those to whom rice is everything, with all other foodstuffs being little more than flavourings, these varieties are as important as the difference between, say, beef and pork to a meat eater.

Seeing the rice-seller was a forceful reminder that I was no longer among city-dwellers, with their 'international' cooking, and that I was getting closer to 'real' Burmese food. Rice aside, perhaps the most fascinating thing about the market was the sheer range of craft-work and antiques on offer: painted folk-puppets, silver jewellery, woven baskets – things hard to find in those places, like Thailand, that have been mobbed by souvenir-hungry visitors. Among the most memorable things about any place where the Burmese congregate are the women and girls, with their cheeks and foreheads smeared with what looks like pale yellow dust. This is a cosmetic made from ground thanaka bark, which protects the skin from the fierce sunlight, though it does turn pretty faces into quite alarming masks.

The evening in Pagan was entrancing. I'd been guided to the Aye Yeiktha Restaurant, which has a terrace overlooking the Shwezigon Pagoda that was lit up and shining white under a full moon – and, yes, the stars did twinkle. That would have been enough but, better still, the food was also good. There was a huge array of small dishes – pork fried with dried chilli, fried aubergine with chilli and shallots, the spicy split-pea fritters the old woman had been eating in the temple, curried this and curried that, and all around the supporting dishes of spicy vegetables. As well as the split-pea fritters, there were a number of other dishes with beans and lentils, which are normally little used in the other countries of the region and which are clearly another borrowing from India. What was very apparent was the taste of peanuts – growing nearby, and used both as an ingredient and as oil. If you wish to add a 'Pagan touch' to the recipes in this section, you could cook with the sort of distinctively flavoured nut oil usually intended for salad dressings, rather than the blander nut cooking oils.

Lacquerware is probably the country's major craft and, on the morning of my departure by car for Mandalay, a visit was organized to the U Ba Nyein Lacquer shop, which is also a school. There I was able to see the delicate hand-painting that produces the intricate traditional patterns, usually red-orange on a shiny black background, for bowls, trays and boxes. The people at the school had kindly laid on a breakfast of sweet coffee with black sticky rice, where the dark-coloured skin is cooked with the grains in coconut and palm sugar. There were also twice-fried beans and deep-fried batter sticks, a Chinese delicacy now eaten all over Asia, usually dipped in sticky-sweet condensed milk – a treat remembered from childhood.

After that, it was off for the long drive over hilly country to the northern capital, where the kings of Myanmar held court before the British arrived. It was a wonderful journey and my one chance to see something of the Burmese countryside, whenever we were able to stop for a rest.

The famous 'Road to Mandalay' of the poem and song is, of course, the river. The actual road doesn't follow the Irrawaddy at all, but heads off inland, starting on the flat river plain, rising into uplands before descending back to level ground as it begins its approach to the city. The journey takes almost a day, but offers a series of intriguing glimpses of Burmese life. We had no sooner left Pagan and were travelling through quite dense patches of forest when we came to a clearing where a large group of bullock carts, perhaps as many as a hundred, were gathered to collect water from a standpipe. Even one such cart is now a rare sight in many parts of Asia, so to stumble on an army of them seemed little short of miraculous. The light brown ridge-backed beasts, two to each cart, were dreamily patient, tails flicking away the flies, as their drivers manipulated them into neat lines to await their turn at the pump. The carts themselves were finely made, with an elegantly curved middle yoke and wavy halters and a fenced platform for the driver and his water container, high above the large wooden wheels. Bullocks are used to pull similarly designed ploughs that turn the rice paddies before the planting season, and many villages

have superb festival carts with sweeping side-rails and elaborately carved halters, with a carved figure balanced on a bar between the two yokes. After each cart had filled up its water tank the driver would urge his team away at a trot, whooping and yelling as they headed for home.

What this sight brought home to me was the main division within Burmese agriculture – the distinct difference between north and south, or Upper and Lower Burma, as they are usually called. Lower Burma, closer to the sea and the river deltas, has always had an easier time because of its abundant rainfall and natural irrigation. Rice is sown in June, transplanted to prevent overcrowding in September, reaped in December or January, and that is that. No manure is needed, beyond the ashes of the stubble which is burned every year. One crop a year is all that is required. In Upper Burma it is a different story. Poor rainfall means that rice must be cultivated in marked-off plots with carefully maintained irrigation ditches and some means of transferring water. When the shoots are about 30cm high and are moved from the nursery plots to the main paddies, they must have a bountiful and constant supply of water or they will yellow and droop.

Later that day we saw this process in action – a group of distant figures out in the flooded fields, men and women, knee-

Nats with placatory offerings

deep in water, bent double plucking up rice shoots for transplanting. While this was a sight you can see anywhere in the East, what made it different was a nearby water wheel, which was lifting water from one side of a restraining dike to the other. Like the carts, this was a carefully made affair of hand-carved spars, holding a wheel about 4m across, with bamboo spokes and a circle of blades. The wheel was operated by a man sitting on a high chair, legs pounding like mad, to keep up the flow. It was an irresistible sight, so it was off with the shoes and socks and into the squelchy mud for a sticky paddle over to the machine. As I could not communicate with the peddler or the planters it was only when I got back to the minibus that the driver was able to explain that this constant irrigation and transplanting were necessary near to Mandalay, where the farmers try to get up to three yearly rice harvests from their limited plots. As this could exhaust the land, they rotate their crops, changing from rice to millet and cotton or maize and beans. They also need some manure, and occasionally turn their buffaloes out on the paddies, which also churns up the land. They call this 'tickling the soil to make it laugh'. The driver didn't seem very fond of Burmese buffaloes, who were, he said, dirty and bad-tempered.

Of course, all these varieties of rice are confined to the relatively low-lying areas of the country. As elsewhere, the hill-tribes in the mountains lead a much more precarious existence, with slash-and-burn agriculture on small clearings, often with poor soil and unpredictable rainfall. This means that they must plant whatever will grow – rice if possible but, if it is too dry, then Indian corn, buckwheat or peas and beans. Although there is considerable variation in cooking among the different tribes, there is some similarity with the food of Northern Thailand and Laos, with the same emphasis on hunted meat and the gathering of wild vegetables and plants. There is also a similar production of charcuterie, such as Shan sausage, one of the few hill-tribe foods that you can find in Rangoon and other lowland cities.

What all the different regions share is a belief in spirits that the Burmese call Nats, and when we continued our journey and stopped for a break at a village we were invited to visit the hall that had been built to house these troublesome figures. You see, Nats are often mischievous, if not downright nasty, and have to be placated or else! Most Southeast Asians believe in spirits – in Thailand, Laos and Cambodia you often see spirit-houses put up as homes for the spirit of the land, lest he get mad because his domain has been usurped. In Burma, though, it goes much further

**Water-wheel beside the road
from Pagan to Mandalay**

**Cleaning a
bespectacled Buddha**

than that. I had already noticed shrines to individual Nats in Rangoon and Pagan, but seeing them all together – there are 37 main Nats – and seeing how important they clearly were to this small village, brought home that this was almost another religion, running parallel with Buddhism.

Some Nats are historical figures, others mythological characters. There are men and women Nats, and each covers a special area of human activity – love, business, health, etc. They are represented by brightly painted and gaudily dressed carved figures, holding the symbols of their power – a sword, some flowers, a silk scarf. Most Nats don't look nasty; many smile, some are quite comic, like figures from a children's story, but that is deceptive and you have to keep them happy with gifts of food and drink and money or they will get back at you.

I bought some bananas at the entrance and went into the long room where they were all lined up, and judiciously picked out any I thought looked a bit tricky, giving each some fruit or sticking a bank note in a hand or inside a costume. The trouble was, I didn't know which was which. I really wanted to get on the right side of the travel Nat in order to ward off any accidents, and I was rather hoping there might be a Nat in charge of food or restaurants; but all I could do was guess. I was told later that there is a Nat who helps out if you eat something bad. The appropriate prayer goes: 'Oh Lord, make the heat of my body go down, let my eating be good and my fever leave.' Which is worth remembering.

Outside, a large bus had drawn up and food sellers were clustered around the travellers, offering them trays of snacks. The Burmese are great eaters of little nibbles – they are on sale everywhere and people consume them all day long, though this doesn't seem to spoil their enthusiasm for the main meals of the day. I noticed the same split-pea fritters I'd seen in Pagan, along with a tray of 'little birds', tiny deep-fried birds that are crunched whole. There was also lots of fried chicken and plenty of fruit, great heaps of bright yellow jackfruit segments as well as baskets of the little sweet bananas. Hawking these snacks is good business for those local people lucky enough to live along the main bus routes. When we stopped at a tiny hamlet a few hours farther on, I saw a man working at a flat griddle, dry-frying brown flat bread, similar to Indian nan. This was clearly a full-time job, supplying the sellers who wait at the roadside. He was fun to watch, skil-

fully tossing his round 'pancakes' in the air so that they landed neatly on his hot-plate.

It was nearly nightfall as we approached Mandalay, but we made one last stop at a village that specializes in brewing palm wine. Tall palm trees surrounded a pretty cluster of dark wooden houses and I could see distant figures running up the thin trees – way, way up under the leaves – to drain away the liquid. This has to be quickly fermented and drunk the same day. The slightly foaming palm wine must be drunk before it turns into a very strong soup that will give a bad headache and an upset stomach the following day. Even fresh, it is very potent and, just off the road, I entered a compound where most of the village menfolk seemed to be lying around in palm wine dreamland, to judge by the absent grins on their faces.

I decided to walk farther on into the village, a place of handsome teakwood houses. The winding paths were lined with the toddy palms, and mango and jackfruit trees. There were more fruit trees around each compound's private vegetable plot, where I saw peas and beans growing, and plenty of large earthenware jars in which river fish would be fermenting, the principal source of flavouring. Indeed, watching the women prepare the evening meal while their husbands got merrily sozzled, I felt very much at home. If this was 'real' Burmese food, it was clearly part of that central Southeast Asian tradition that I had seen all through my travels – plenty of rice, curried catfish from the nearby stream and some

**Novice monk near
Lake Inle**

highly spiced stir-fried watercress picked at the water's edge. The principal tastes are garlic and fermented or pickled fish, and there is plentiful use of turmeric – the main source of gingery flavour in Burmese food – which also gives many dishes their typical orange-yellow hue.

The village had a Nat shrine at its centre – just three Nats this time, all with reassuring smiles on their faces. Still, I gave them a bow and a bank note before we headed off on the last stage of what had proved an amazing journey.

There is no doubt that Mandalay, with its famous temples and its relics of Burma's royal past, is one of those dream destinations that every serious traveller hopes to see one day. Indeed it would have been the high spot of my visit if I hadn't already been to Pagan, after which nothing could ever compete. I seriously advise future visitors to the country to go first to Mandalay, then down to Pagan, which should be the very last place you visit in

Burma. Happily, the visit to Mandalay was redeemed by a spectacular event that was totally unexpected and all the better for it. I had gone to the Maha Muni Pagoda to see the huge, gold, seated statue of the Buddha, which is getting bigger by the minute, thanks to a constant stream of men who buy little sheets of gold leaf that they smear on to the enormous figure. They can put their gold wherever they wish, except on the face, and can climb up and walk behind it, to reach up to the top of the head. It is a strange and mysterious sight, to see the little gilded flakes shimmering on the vast body. No one knows exactly how much precious metal has been stuck to the Buddha over the years, but the effect is awesome. Oddly enough, among the few examples of modern technology I saw in use in Burma were the television cameras strategically arranged around the statue so that female worshippers, who may not climb up behind the statue, can still have an all-round view of proceedings on television sets placed about the temple.

It was as I was leaving the building that the great event happened. I suddenly found myself engulfed in a procession of fabulously clothed merrymakers, all in traditional costume. Groups of family and friends surrounded the doll-like figures of young boys dressed in white robes with coloured head-dresses, going into the local monastery to be novice monks during the rains. I had stumbled on a Shinpyu Ceremony, when boys aged seven and upwards become temporary monks at the beginning of the Buddhist New Year – their sisters get their ears pierced! It was a sumptuous spectacle, with those who could afford it paying for their sons to ride on richly caparisoned elephants. This was the India of the Maharajas – a reminder that Buddhism originally came from India and Sri Lanka, bringing so many other traditions with it, many of them Hindu in origin. The supporters wore coloured turbans and costumes embroidered with gold and beads, while the little novices were shaded by fringed silk parasols, the mahouts carefully directing their swaying beasts, as those below played instruments and clapped and shouted and danced alongside.

I wished I could follow them, aware that there would be a monster feast at some point in all the celebrations, and aware too that I would certainly have been invited to join in, because one always is. I was told later that rich families, like those who had hired the elephants, always offer at least four meat dishes and four fish and seafood, as well as vegetables, soup and rice. Middle-class families might get an Indian caterer to make a large meat and rice platter, while poorer families would just offer a rice and a curry dish with some pickles. I have to admit I would have followed an elephant if I could, but I had friends waiting at the Sa Khan Thar, which I had been told was Mandalay's best restaurant and where the owner Daw Kin Ma Lay was waiting to welcome me.

We ate outside under an enormous tamarind tree, its furry pods dangling down like Christmas decorations. Before the meal, Daw Kin Ma Lay took me into her kitchen, where a line of cooks was furiously at work, chopping and stir-frying, Daw Kin Ma Lay is one of the new breed of Burmese businesswomen who, like my friend in Rangoon, are trying to get the country ready to rejoin the

Nun reading a Buddhist text in Sagaing

world community. The Sa Khan Thar is one of the rare places where you can eat the sort of Burmese food normally found only in private houses, and that night we had a feast which ranged over the whole spectrum of flavours that encompasses Burma's Indian and Southeast Asian roots. There were fried sweetcorn cakes with crispy shallots at one end of the spectrum, crispy fried duck at the other, with hints of Thailand in a hot-and-sour fish cake salad. One of my friends went out to the street, where a travelling pickle-seller was offering mixtures of sweet-and-sour pickled fruits – mango, rose apple and a bitter fruit halfway between a plum and an olive – from large, wonderfully coloured glass jars, set up on a hand-drawn wagon.

As I feasted under the stars in Mandalay, it was clear to me that such food could be immensely popular outside Burma. I can see it finding great success in those countries like Britain that have already learned to love Indian and Chinese food – with Burmese food you get both, and more. For the moment it is virtually impossible to eat true Burmese food outside the country, except for the occasional restaurant in California. Of course, the first step is for the Burmese themselves to perfect the art of serving a domestic cuisine to a passing public, and with the likes of Daw Kin Ma Lay that is starting to happen. Next will be the moment when the world discovers Burma itself – and with Pagan on offer that is certainly going to happen. Until then, this unique food – like its country of origin – will have to remain one of the world's great secrets.

WET TAUK-TAUK GYAW
PORK FRIED WITH DRIED CHILLI

INGREDIENTS
- 2 tablespoons oil
- 2 garlic cloves, finely chopped
- 2 large dried red chillies, coarsely chopped
- 115g (4oz) pork, thinly sliced
- 60g (2oz) cauliflower, cut into small florets
- 60g (2oz) carrots, thinly sliced
- 1 tablespoon fish sauce
- 1 tablespoon light soy sauce
- ½ teaspoon sugar
- 2 spring onions, finely chopped

I ate this in Pagan, on the Aye Yeiktha Restaurant terrace with its spectacular view across to the illuminated Shwezigon Pagoda. This is a full dish for a main meal and should be served with a number of vegetable side-dishes, like the Bamboo Shoots Stir-fried with Spice Paste (page 149) and the Fried Sweetcorn with Crispy Shallots (see below).

PREPARATION

Heat the oil in a wok or deep frying pan and fry the garlic until golden. Add the chillies and stir briefly. Add the pork and stir-fry until almost cooked through.

Add all the remaining vegetables in succession, stirring once between each addition. Add the fish sauce, soy sauce and sugar, and stir briefly.

Remove from the heat and quickly stir in the spring onions. Turn out on a plate and serve.

PYAUNG-BU GYAW
FRIED SWEETCORN WITH CRISPY SHALLOTS

INGREDIENTS
- 3 cobs of fresh sweetcorn
- 2 tablespoons oil
- 6 small shallots, thinly sliced
- Salt and pepper

This was one of several delicious 'side dishes' served by Daw Kin Ma Lay at the Sa Khan Thar Restaurant in Mandalay. It goes especially well with Daw Kin Ma Lay's Crispy Duck (see page 154) and the Burmese Hot Sauce (see page 146).

PREPARATION

Using a large sharp knife and setting the cobs on their ends, remove the sweetcorn kernels from the uncooked cobs, Set aside.

Heat the oil in a frying pan which has a tight-fitting lid and fry the shallots until crispy. Remove, drain and set aside.

Reheat the oil, add the sweetcorn and stir. Cover the pan and cook until the corn softens, about 5 minutes.

Remove from the heat, add the crispy shallots and season to taste with salt and pepper. Turn out on a dish and serve.

NGA-PE THOKE
HOT-AND-SOUR FISH CAKE SALAD

INGREDIENTS

- I large dried red chilli, finely chopped
- I teaspoon finely chopped fresh turmeric
- I teaspoon finely chopped garlic
- I tablespoon finely chopped shallot
- ¼ teaspoon salt
- 450g (Ilb) white fish fillets (such as cod, monkfish, etc.), broken into flakes
- A mixture of assorted salad vegetables, such as shredded lettuce leaves, onion rings, cucumber slices, tomato wedges, chopped spring onions and coriander leaves, to serve

FOR THE DRESSING:

- 3 tablespoons fish sauce
- 3 tablespoons lime juice
- I tablespoon sugar
- 4 small fresh red or green chillies, finely chopped

PREPARATION

In a mortar, pound together the chilli, turmeric, garlic and shallot to make a paste. Add the salt, then add the flakes of fish and pound together. Using your fingers, divide the paste in two and mould both halves into a sausage shape.

Place in the upper compartment of a steamer and steam for 15-20 minutes, until solid.

While the fishcake is steaming, make the dressing: mix all the ingredients in a bowl.

When the fishcake is cooked, remove and cut into slices about 5mm (¼in) thick. Arrange the salad vegetables on a serving platter. Arrange the fish cake slices on top and either pour the dressing over the salad, tossing well, or serve it in a separate bowl for diners to use as they wish.

NGAN-BYA-YE DHYAW
BURMESE HOT SAUCE

INGREDIENTS

- I tablespoon oil
- I tablespoon finely chopped fresh turmeric
- I tablespoon dried shrimp, pounded to powder
- I teaspoon chilli powder
- 3 tablespoons fish sauce

PREPARATION

Heat the oil in a wok or deep frying pan and briefly fry the turmeric. Add the powdered shrimp and briefly stir-fry again.

Remove from the heat and add the chilli powder and fish sauce. Stir, turn into a dipping bowl and serve.

MON-LA-DOKE-THOKE
WHITE CABBAGE SALAD

INGREDIENTS

- 225g (8oz) white cabbage
- I onion, thinly sliced
- 2 small fresh red chillies, finely chopped
- ½ teaspoon salt
- I tablespoon lime juice
- I tablespoon peanut (groundnut) oil
- I tablespoon dried shrimp, pounded to powder

PREPARATION

Chop the white cabbage into thin rounds, then break these up with your fingers so that they fall apart into small twisted pieces. Place them in a bowl. Add the other ingredients and stir well.

PAZUN HIN
PRAWN CURRY

INGREDIENTS
- 2 tablespoons oil
- 30g (1oz) onion, coarsely chopped
- 175g (6oz) raw prawns, peeled and deveined
- 1 tablespoon fish sauce
- 1 teaspoon ground turmeric
- ½ teaspoon sugar
- ¼ teaspoon salt
- 85g (3oz) tomatoes, cut into wedges
- Coriander leaves to garnish

This was one of the main dishes served at the home of my friend in Rangoon. To enjoy it 'Burmese-style', you should accompany it with spicy vegetable side dishes, such as Bamboo Shoots Stir-fried with Spice Paste and Tomato Salad (see below) and Twice-Cooked Split-peas (see page 154).

PREPARATION

Heat the oil in a wok or frying pan. Add the onion and stir, add all the other ingredients except the coriander in succession, stirring once between each addition. Turn out on a plate, garnish with coriander leaves and serve.

HMYIT-KYAW
BAMBOO SHOOTS STIR-FRIED WITH SPICE PASTE

INGREDIENTS
- 2 garlic cloves, finely chopped
- 4 small shallots, finely chopped
- 1 teaspoon finely chopped fresh turmeric
- 2 tablespoons oil
- 175g (6oz) bamboo shoots, thinly sliced
- ½ teaspoon salt

Although this is served with the main meal, it is a side dish. There should always be several of such side dishes accompanying a full Burmese meal.

PREPARATION

In a mortar, pound together the garlic, shallots and turmeric to make a paste.

Heat the oil in a wok or deep frying pan. Stir in the paste, add the bamboo shoots and stir-fry briefly.

Add the salt, stir once, then turn out on a dish and serve.

KHAYAN-GYIN-THI-THOKE
TOMATO SALAD

INGREDIENTS
- 2 tablespoons oil
- 3 garlic cloves, thinly sliced
- 4 small shallots, thinly sliced
- 225g (8oz) tomatoes, cut into wedges
- 1 medium onion, coarsely chopped
- 2 tablespoons crushed peanuts
- 1 tablespoon finely chopped coriander leaves

PREPARATION

Heat the oil in a wok or deep frying pan and fry the garlic and shallots until crispy. Remove, drain, retaining the oil, and set aside.

Place the tomatoes, onion and crushed peanuts in a bowl. Once the reserved oil has cooled, pour it over the contents of the bowl and stir well.

Add the reserved crispy garlic and shallot. Stir once, sprinkle with chopped coriander leaves and serve.

NGAR-ASAT-KYAW
FRIED FISH WITH CRISPY CHILLI, GARLIC AND SHALLOTS

INGREDIENTS

- 1 teaspoon ground turmeric
- 1 whole medium-sized firm-fleshed fish, filleted and cut into 2.5cm (1in) pieces
- 2 tablespoons oil
- 4 small shallots, thinly sliced
- 2 garlic cloves, thinly sliced
- 2 large dried red chillies, coarsely chopped
- Oil for deep-frying
- 2 teaspoons salt
- ½ teaspoon sugar

PREPARATION

Use trout or sea bass for this dish Sprinkle the turmeric over the fish pieces and leave to marinate for 20 minutes. Meanwhile, heat the 2 tablespoons of oil in a wok or deep frying pan and fry the shallots until crispy. Remove, drain and set aside. Repeat the process with the garlic and the chillies. Reserve the oil. Heat the oil for deep-frying and fry the marinated fish until golden. Remove and drain. Reheat the reserved first oil in the wok or deep frying pan. Add the deep-fried fish and stir. Add the crispy shallots, garlic and chilli, and stir. Add the salt and sugar, and stir. Turn out on a plate and serve.

HKAYAN-THI PYOT-KYAW
FRIED AUBERGINE WITH CHILLI AND SHALLOTS

INGREDIENTS

- 4 small fresh red or green chillies
- 2 garlic cloves
- 4 small shallots
- 2 tablespoons oil
- 225g (8oz) aubergine, quartered lengthways, then cut into large cubes
- ½ teaspoon salt
- 1 teaspoon sugar
- 3 tablespoons vegetable stock (see page 14)

PREPARATION

In a mortar, pound the chillies, garlic and shallots to make a paste. In a frying pan which has a matching tight-fitting lid, heat the oil and stir in the paste. Add the aubergine and stir (well for green, less for black). Flavour with the salt and sugar, add the stock and stir. Cover and cook for up to 5 minutes, depending on which type of aubergine is being used. Turn out on a dish and serve.

THAKHWA-THI HIN-GYO
CUCUMBER AND DRIED SHRIMP SOUP

INGREDIENTS

- 2 tablespoons small dried shrimps
- 1 teaspoon shrimp paste (see page 14)
- 1 litre (1¾ pints) vegetable stock (see page 14)
- 2 tablespoons oil
- 1 garlic clove, finely chopped
- ½ teaspoon finely chopped fresh turmeric
- 225g (8oz) cucumber, peeled and finely diced
- 2 tablespoons fish sauce
- ½ teaspoon sugar
- ½ teaspoon pepper

PREPARATION

In a mortar, pound half the dried shrimps to a powder, reserving the other half. In a bowl, mix the shrimp paste with 2 tablespoons of the vegetable stock and set aside. In a large pan, heat the oil and fry the garlic and turmeric until the garlic is golden. Pour the remainder of the stock into the pan and mix. Add the cucumber, the reserved dried shrimps and the powdered dried shrimps, then stir in the shrimp paste and the remaining vegetable stock. Add the fish sauce, sugar and pepper. Bring to the boil and serve immediately.

WET-THA KHAUK-SWE-GYAW
STIR-FRIED NOODLES WITH PORK

INGREDIENTS

* 2 tablespoons oil
* 2 garlic cloves, finely chopped
* 1 teaspoon finely chopped ginger
* 1 large dried red chilli, coarsely chopped
* 225g (8oz) pork, thinly sliced
* 1 medium onion, finely chopped
* 1 tablespoon fish sauce
* 1 tablespoon light soy sauce
* 1 teaspoon sugar
* 225g (8oz) medium flat white flour noodles, soaked and drained (see page 11)
* 115g (4oz) celery, coarsely chopped

There is a large, two-storey dragon boat permanently moored in the moat that surrounds the remains of the Royal Palace in Mandalay. Used as a restaurant, it is more of a curiosity than a gourmet's paradise, but this variation of a classic Asian noodle dish was a happy choice for me when I visited the establishment.

PREPARATION

Heat the oil in a wok or deep frying pan and fry the garlic until golden.

Add the ginger and stir. Add the chilli and stir. Then add the pork and stir well until it is just cooked through.

Add the onion and stir. Add the fish sauce, soy sauce and sugar, and stir once. Then add the noodles and stir well for 1 minute.

Add the celery, stir briefly, turn out on a plate and serve.

BAYAGYAW
SPICY SPLIT-PEA FRITTERS

INGREDIENTS

* 115g (4oz) dried yellow split-peas, soaked overnight
* 1 medium onion, finely chopped
* 2 small fresh red chillies, finely chopped
* 2 kaffir lime leaves, finely chopped
* 1 tablespoon finely chopped coriander (leaf and stem)
* ½ teaspoon ground turmeric
* ½ teaspoon salt
* 1 tablespoon cornflour
* Oil for deep-frying

This dish can be used as a starter, though it is often served with drinks and may even appear with afternoon tea or coffee. It was the 'snack' the old lady had brought to the temple in Pagan, but it can be one of the 'side dishes' served with a curry.

PREPARATION

Drain the split-peas and place them in a bowl with 4 tablespoons water and all the other ingredients except the oil. Mix thoroughly to form a paste.

Heat the oil for deep-frying. Scoop up a heap of paste in one teaspoon and use a second to ease it into the hot oil. Repeat until all the paste has been used and all the oval pellets have been fried until golden brown, cooking in batches if necessary. Remove and drain the fritters as they are cooked, and serve immediately.

SEIK-THA HIN
LAMB WITH MINT LEAVES

INGREDIENTS

- 450g (1lb) lamb steaks, cubed
- ¼ teaspoon salt
- 1 teaspoon ground turmeric
- 2 tablespoons oil
- 2 garlic cloves, finely chopped
- ½ teaspoon ground cumin
- 1 medium onion, coarsely chopped
- 2 medium tomatoes, coarsely chopped
- 2 tablespoons fish sauce
- ½ teaspoon sugar
- 2 medium fresh red chillies, coarsely chopped
- 20 fresh mint leaves

PREPARATION

Place the lamb, salt and turmeric in a large pan with 225ml (8fl oz) water and bring to the boil. Cover and simmer for 1 hour.

Heat the oil in a wok or deep frying pan and fry the garlic until golden. Stir in the cumin.

Remove the meat from the water, drain well and add to the frying pan. Stir well, then add the onion, tomatoes, fish sauce, sugar and chillies, continuing to stir.

Remove from the heat, quickly stir in the mint leaves and serve.

PE-GYAN-GYAW
TWICE-COOKED SPLIT-PEAS

INGREDIENTS

- 175g (6oz) dried yellow split-peas, soaked overnight
- 2 tablespoons oil
- 2 garlic cloves, finely chopped
- 1 tablespoon finely chopped ginger
- 1 medium onion, coarsely chopped
- Salt to taste

PREPARATION

Remove the split-peas from their soaking water, transfer to a pan of fresh boiling water and simmer for 5 minutes. Remove, drain and set aside.

Heat the oil in a wok or deep frying pan and fry the garlic until golden. Add the ginger and briefly stir-fry. Add the onion and briefly stir-fry.

Add the split-peas and a sprinkling of salt to taste. Stir-fry for 2 minutes, then turn out on a plate and serve.

BE-GIN
CRISPY DUCK

INGREDIENTS

- 1 whole duck, about 1.85kg (4lb)
- 2 tablespoons five-spice powder
- 1 teaspoon salt
- ½ teaspoon pepper
- 1 teaspoon sugar
- Oil for deep-frying

PREPARATION

Evenly coat the duck inside and out with five-spice powder, salt, pepper and sugar. Place in the upper compartment of a steamer and steam for 15 minutes. Remove and let any water drain away.

With a Chinese axe or chopper, halve the duck lengthways and chop away the wings and legs. Then chop each half into small portions, roughly 2.5cm (1in) wide. Heat the oil and deep-fry the duck pieces until crispy. Remove them as they are cooked, drain well and serve.

AMETHA HIN

BEEF IN TAMARIND SAUCE

INGREDIENTS

- 2 medium dried red chillies, finely chopped
- 1 teaspoon finely chopped ginger
- 2 garlic cloves, finely chopped
- 6 small shallots, finely chopped
- 2 tablespoons oil
- 450g (1lb) beef, cubed
- 1 teaspoon ground turmeric
- 2 tablespoons fish sauce
- 2 tablespoons tamarind water (see page 19)

PREPARATION

In a mortar, pound together the chillies, ginger, garlic and shallots to form a paste.

Heat the oil and stir in the paste. Add the beef and stir well. Add the turmeric and fish sauce, and stir well. Add 350ml (12fl oz) water and bring back to the boil. Cover and simmer for 1 hour.

Finally, add the tamarind water, stir and simmer for a further 5 minutes. Turn out into a bowl and serve.

KYET-THA KHAUK-SWE-BYOKE

BURMESE CHICKEN NOODLE

INGREDIENTS

- 2 tablespoons oil
- 225ml (8fl oz) coconut milk
- 275g (10oz) chicken, thinly sliced
- 450ml (¾ pint) chicken stock (see page 14)
- 225g (8oz) egg noodles (see page 11)
- 2 tablespoons fish sauce
- 1 teaspoon sugar
- 1 tablespoon lemon juice

FOR THE CURRY PASTE:

- ½ teaspoon coriander seeds
- 1 teaspoon finely chopped fresh turmeric
- 1 teaspoon finely chopped ginger
- 1 large dried red chilli, finely chopped
- 3 small red shallots, finely chopped
- ¼ teaspoon salt

This is the classic Burmese noodle dish, one of the rare Burmese recipes known outside the country. It brings together perfectly many of the different influences that are part of Burmese cuisine. As I learned on my visit, there are considerable variations in how this national noodle dish is served. At the River View Restaurant in Pagan it was an elaborate affair in which most of the ingredients were served separately and mixed by the diners. This is the simple 'all-in-one' version I ate in Rangoon's Bogyoke Aung San Market.

You will need only 1 tablespoon of the curry paste for this dish; the rest will keep for several days in the refrigerator and can be used for many other dishes.

PREPARATION

First make the curry paste: in a mortar, pound the coriander seeds to a powder. Then add each ingredient in turn, pounding together to make a paste. Stir in the salt and set aside.

Heat the oil in a wok or deep frying pan and stir in 1 tablespoon of the curry paste. Add the coconut milk and stir well. Add the chicken and cook, stirring, until the meat is just cooked through.

Pour in the stock and bring back to the boil. Add the noodles and stir well. Add the fish sauce and sugar and stir well.

Remove from the heat and add the lemon juice. Stir once, pour into a bowl and serve.

KYAUK-KYAW

JELLY CUSTARD

INGREDIENTS

- 115g (4oz) agar agar jelly powder (see page 19)
- 225g (8oz) sugar
- 450ml (¾ pint) coconut milk
- 1 egg

This is a basic recipe that you can vary at will – the agar jelly is tasteless, so you can add sweet or savoury flavours to it. I've used coconut here, but I've come across flavours as varied as the juice squeezed from banyan leaves to instant coffee! More conventionally, you could replace the coconut milk with orange juice – or other fruit juices – and you could put a little chopped fruit into the moulds before pouring in the jelly.

PREPARATION

Put the agar agar jelly powder into a saucepan with 450ml (¾ pint) water and bring to the boil, stirring constantly.

Add the sugar and stir well. Add the coconut milk and stir as you bring back to the boil. Beat the egg and stir into the mixture. Simmer for a moment, then pour into moulds. Leave to set and cool.

Turn out (a quick dip in hot water will help) and serve.

MON-LET-SAUNG

SAGO WITH PALM SUGAR AND COCONUT MILK

INGREDIENTS

- 225ml (8fl oz) dried sago
- 450ml (¾ pint) coconut milk
- 225g (8oz) palm sugar (see page 19)

PREPARATION

Wash the sago in cold water and drain.

In a pan, heat 450ml (¾ pint) fresh water. Add the sago and bring to the boil. When the sago floats to the surface, it is cooked. Remove with a slotted spoon as it rises and place in a bowl of cold water.

When all the sago is transferred, remove from the cold water and drain. Place in a serving bowl and set aside.

In a saucepan, heat the coconut milk. Add the palm sugar and stir until dissolved, then transfer to another serving bowl.

Serve the sago and this warm sauce separately, allowing diners to mix them as they wish. In summer the sago can be served cold with crushed ice.

Malaysia an

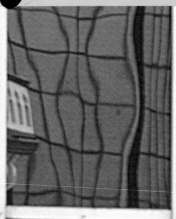

d Singapore

TOMORROW TODAY

When the railway line running south from Bangkok was finally completed, early in the 20th century, it brought to an end centuries of division and conflict by linking Thailand to its southern neighbour, the then British colony of Malaya. At the time, it was a miracle of engineering, running from the banks of the Chao Phya River, across the narrow isthmus of southern Thailand to the Andaman Sea, through dense jungle and water-logged rice paddies, on across the border, skirting the Cameron Highlands to Kuala Lumpur, for the final leg over the Straits of Jahore to Singapore Island.

Poultry seller, Central Market, Kota Bharu, Malaysia

It was no easy ride and even today the journey still takes three days and nights, with travellers needing to bring their own supplies to augment the limited meals available on board. The coming of aircraft made this seem even more arduous, reducing the train's customers to the very poor, the occasional backpacker from Europe and the few who were just passionate about railways and who could still see the charm of the Victorian fretwork stations dotted along the line, as if little fantasy English villages had been set down right in the middle of Asia.

All that changed in 1993 when the company that runs the Orient Express, the luxury train that travels between London and Venice, decided to put something similar, the Eastern and Oriental Express, on the old Thailand-Malaysia line. Carriages were fitted with rosewood and mahogany cabins and suites, with lamps by Lalique and Baccarat crystal for the dining rooms and bars. There were leather armchairs for the library and the train was staffed with chefs, waiters, traditional dancers and even a fortune-teller, to help the 36 hours from Bangkok to Singapore pass without a dull moment.

Despite its drawbacks, I was one of the few who loved the old train. I used to travel from Bangkok's Hua Lampong Station, with its high arches and Italianate tile floors, on the four-hour journey to the tiny gingerbread station at Hua Hin on the eastern coast, the prettiest of all the stations because it served the King's seaside villa. Even I have to admit, however, that the luxuries of having breakfast in bed off a silver tray in my own cabin aboard the new train, or drinking cocktails on the open observation deck at nightfall, take some beating.

The food on board is supervised by head chef Kevin Cape, who is based in Bangkok where he is able to stock up with fresh ingredients just before the train leaves. If there is anything special on offer at any of the stations, he can buy more en route. The meals served are a mix of Eastern and Western ideas, the sort of blend that in recent years has enlivened the cooking of many young chefs in London, New York and California. Today, there are few leading cooks who don't find some use for lemon grass and chillies, and I've included in this chapter a beancurd soup from the train's menu that shows how delicious this sort of inventiveness can be. There is nothing inauthentic about this type of cooking — indeed the region of southern Thailand that the train crosses is famous for its blend of Thai and Malaysian cooking styles.

Malaysian food, like the country and its people, is an intricate web of world-wide influences born of its strategic position astride the main sea route linking Europe, Arabia, India, China and the Far East. It was the Port of Malacca (present day Melaka) on the western coast of the peninsula that drew spice traders from Europe, following where the Indians had led. Indian traders were visiting the peninsula early in the Christian era and by the end of the 13th century AD Muslim voyagers from the sub-continent had brought Islam, the dominant religion of modern Malaysia.

Two centuries later, Malacca had fallen to the Portuguese and by 1641 to the Dutch. They were finally out-manoeuvred at the end of the 18th century when the British set up a rival port on the island of Penang, which quickly replaced Malacca as the main centre of the Southeast Asian trade route. Initially the British were interested only in these coastal trading ports, establishing another settlement at Singapore. Gradually, however, the inland sultanates were drawn into agreements and unions, and by the early years of the 20th century the entire peninsula was effectively transformed into a colony. This in turn, drew tens of thousands of

Chinese immigrants as coolie labour, and others came later as traders, until they were almost as numerous as the original Malays.

Only an outside power could have held this volatile mix together, but the humiliating defeat by the invading Japanese in 1942 shattered the illusion of British invincibility. When the war ended and colonial rule was re-established, it was only a question of time before independence would come, though there was still a protracted jungle war against communist insurgents and a great deal of manoeuvring to satisfy the claims and fears of the different communities before the present state of harmony was achieved.

Today there are two separate nations: Malaysia and Singapore. Malaysia consists of the original peninsula, now joined by the two states that occupy the northern rim of the island of Borneo across the South China Sea – Sabah and Sarawak, once ruled by the descendants of the British adventurer James Brooke, the 'White Raja'. The second state, wealthy and successful far beyond its tiny dimensions, is the island-city of Singapore. Its predominantly Chinese population made continuing relations with the increasingly Malay-dominated state to the north difficult – with it eventually separating from the union in 1965.

Whatever their political differences, Malaysia and Singapore have much in common. Both have such a variety of cultures and religions that they celebrate New Year four times a year and both share a range of culinary influences that is almost a history of world food. In the simplest terms, true Malaysian cooking is rich and aromatic, heavily spiced but lightened with herb flavours,

tamarind sourness and fish saltiness taken from its northern neighbours. This mix is easiest seen in the ubiquitous satay, a dish that clearly echoes the Arabic kebab, though its accompanying peanut sauce merges Indian spices with Southeast Asian herb and fish flavours. In the main centres, especially independent Singapore, later waves of Indian and Chinese immigrants have remained loyal to the culinary traditions of their places of origin, so that the visitor is offered a wide choice – from Malay cooking to Cantonese and Kashmiri cuisine, or even an English steak and kidney pudding if you so desire.

Of course, most first-time visitors to Malaysia see only the main sites of the Western Peninsula, where the population is divided 60/30 between ethnic Malays and Malay-Chinese, with the remaining 10 per cent of Indian origin. It is the food of the two largest groups that most interests me, especially when they come together. Many Chinese arrived in the region in the late 18th and early 19th centuries, subsequently settling and marrying Malay or Indonesian wives. These 'Straits' or 'Baba' Chinese lived in two worlds, their descendants – the 'Peranakan' or 'children of mixed race' – even more so. Their homes looked Chinese and they wore Chinese clothes, but the food they ate was nonya, the word for their mother, who followed her own Malay culinary traditions with a leavening of Chinese recipes introduced to please her husband.

Bullock cart, Malaysia

Nonya food is one of the great cuisines of Asia, but is hard to find outside Peranakan homes. Even there it is thought to be dying out, as the modern descendants of the settlers have started to veer either to their Chinese or to their Malay ancestry, abandoning the middle ground. Nonya cooking has two main centres – Singapore, of course, but also Penang, the tiny island off the north-west coast of the peninsula, where the Eastern and Oriental Express makes its first long stop on the journey south.

As the train pulled into Butterworth Station on the mainland we were greeted by drums, bells and a Chinese lion weaving its dance of welcome. Penang is a 15-minute ferry ride across the narrow straits to Georgetown, which, as its name suggests, was a British creation – now largely inhabited by Chinese, or rather their Peranakan descendants, whose culture dominates the island. Acquired by Captain Francis Light in 1786 as a trading post for the East India Company, it was named for the future King George IV. The tiny town was established during one of the best periods in British architecture, which has left the gracious sea-front centre around Fort Cornwallis fringed with elegant white Regency and Georgian porticoes.

This was the setting for the brief tour that the train passengers were able to make. As I had already visited the island some years earlier, I could also recall the Chinese quarter, with its fabulous carved and coloured temples and Clan Houses, heavy with incense, and the line of somewhat shabby but still imposing Chinese merchants' mansions along Millionaire's Row, on the way to the best beaches and the new tourist hotels. My happiest memories were of animals in public places: the snakes, some of them poisonous, roaming more or less freely round the bluntly named Snake Temple, and the tribes of mischievous macaque monkeys fighting for control of territory in the Botanic Gardens.

Georgetown itself has a little museum in what was once a British school and when I visited it in the late eighties it had an appealingly faded air. There were few other visitors to share my fascination with the collection of photographs and souvenirs of turn-of-the-century Penang. At the rear of the building were room settings and costumes that showed something of Peranakan life – the Baba and Nonya in their long embroidered Chinese wedding robes, and the sort of inlaid lacquered furniture that I then thought unique. Since my visit to Hoi An in Vietnam, however, I now know this to be part of a shared culture that these intrepid Chinese travellers spread all round the South China Sea, in the trading ports where they settled, leading a new life while still haunted by the old one that they had left behind.

The food they created could still be enjoyed on Gurney Drive after nightfall, where restaurants and food stalls offered everything from 'pure' Indian, Chinese and Malay dishes to the nonya versions that drew on all these traditions to create something unique. There is a distinct difference between the two centres of nonya

The statue of Singapore's founder, Sir Stamford Raffles, surrounded by the towering symbols of the city's success

cooking: in Singapore the use of creamy coconut milk sauces and a slightly heavier hand with dry spices shows the influence of southern Malay and Indonesian traditions; by contrast Penang has more of the sour lemon/lime tastes of neighbouring Thailand, and sauces are lighter and more liquid. Both these traditions merge in Laksa Lemak, the noodle dish strongly flavoured with coconut milk (see page 170), that veers towards India with hints of tamarind and turmeric, then back East with fish sauce and shrimp paste. Penang and Singapore have their own versions of the dish and in Penang you should try Penang laksa, with fish.

Sadly, there was no time to repeat that treat, though we did take a brief rickshaw ride around the town before going back on board the train for afternoon tea. This very English custom still lives on in Malaysia. The railway line skirts the Cameron Highlands and the tea plantations where the British settled, and where their friends used to come for a break from the tropical heat of Kuala Lumpur. In the midst of dense jungle inhabited by tribal peoples who, if the warning signs by the side of the highway are to be believed, still capture and kill anyone foolish enough to stray from the main roads, the British built a dream world of mock-Tudor hotels. Some years ago, I stayed at Ye Olde Smokehouse with its log fires, horse brasses and inglenooks, where I found Devon cream teas with scones and strawberry jam. Today, Malaysian families still drive up for tea and have themselves photographed in front of these eccentric reminders of a way of life that now seems barely credible.

The same is true of Kuala Lumpur railway station, where the train made a brief midnight stopover, just long enough to see the British imagination at its most fantastical. This time the architecture is an astonishing mix of Arabic, Gothic and Greek. It is a fitting prelude to the city itself, for 'KL', as everybody calls it, is built around a cricket pitch, the pedang, with a mock-Tudor clubhouse. There, men in whites bowl and bat and ignore the fact that enormous skyscrapers – mighty symbols of the rocketing success of this 'tiger' economy – now loom over their village green. Even religion has been caught up in the drive for growth. One of the city's finest modern creations is the Masjid Negara, the National Mosque, a vast construction that can accommodate hundreds of worshippers at Friday prayers. A mountain of shoes piles up at the entrances, as the men in their sarongs and songkok caps face Mecca in unison, the air cooled by shimmering pools of water whose reflections play on the marble walls and tiled floors.

Like the other capitals of the free-wheeling Asian economies, KL has enjoyed almost unbelievable growth, though it has been lucky to have a solid infrastructure laid out in the colonial era. As in Rangoon, there are gardens and parks and flower beds, good basic sanitation and a manageable road system. Far from being oppressive, squalid and polluted, the city still feels cool and relatively open.

So where do you eat in KL? In a revolving restaurant at the top of a tower? In the cavernous dining room of an international hotel? No, you go to a car park! Every night when the vehicles and buses have gone, an army of hawkers appears with little metal tables and chairs to convert the Jalan Benteng Car Park into the city's biggest restaurant, with lines and lines of stalls lit by dangling kerosene lamps, mostly offering Malay or Muslim Indian food. As with nonya cooking, Malaysian cuisine is divided between north and south, with the area nearest to Thailand having similar sour flavours and lighter, liquid sauces, while the south has the thicker, spicier, coconut-rich dishes that echo India and Indonesia.

To complete the impression that this is one part of the city which has refused to grow up, diners can look across the River Klang to the older Masjid Jame Mosque, with its Moorish minarets and crenellations – a vision of KL before the skyscrapers. The food, too, is traditional Malay, for this is certainly the place to find those myriad snacks and appetizers that are the great feature of the country's cuisine. There are dozens of varieties of satay, with almost anything that can be threaded on a stick and grilled. The satay sellers are everywhere, their sticks far longer, with less meat, than you find elsewhere, though you get a very large bunch with every order. To make the best of what's on offer, you need rice and one substantial plate like a beef rendang, originally a Sumatran dish, but now a fixed part of the Malay repertoire, the meat strongly flavoured with seed spices, enlivened with ginger and galangal. With this you should order at least two sambals – spicy side-dishes which are sometimes eaten alone – their strong flavours enabling a hungry diner to consume great quantities of plain rice. I remember an egg sambal with lots of chilli and shallots, and a similar fish sambal that also had lemon grass and tamarind.

That brief stopover on the train brought it all back, the smells of frying garlic and chilli, the appetite rising with each new dish, no matter how much one seemed to have eaten. Now it was off on the final stage of our journey, overnight to Singapore. The train ride had been an enjoyable interlude, though it was our fellow passengers who provided most of the entertainment. One woman had hired a separate cabin for her baggage and changed her clothes almost hourly. By dinner on our last evening she was given a round of applause each time she appeared in a new outfit and when, during the meal, her neighbour accidentally spilt some wine on her dress and she dashed off to change yet again, her husband told the man not to worry as the accident had 'made her very happy!'

I woke at dawn, in time for coffee as we passed over the causeway to the island and the shock of the new. KL may be modern, but Singapore is ultramodern. This is the architecture of the future, set amongst parks and gardens, and so impeccably clean even the sides of the railway track seem to have been given a wash and brush up. Inevitably this has produced a reaction: Singapore is said to be too clean, too regimented, too authoritarian. There are fines for dropping litter, fines for spitting and the result, so critics insist, is boring. Well, not for me. To come from the squalor of Bangkok to the modern miracle that is Singapore is a journey from Hell to Heaven.

Perhaps aware that the push for tomorrow may have gone too far, the authorities are now trying to save and restore some of the survivors of an earlier age: China Town, the Indian Quarter

and the imposing Imperial buildings that still nestle, down among the skyscraper banks and department stores. Happily they seem to have come to this conclusion just in time and you can see the results if you stand by the statue of Singapore's founder, Sir Stamford Raffles, on North Boat Quay at the mouth of the Singapore River.

In 1819, Raffles negotiated the treaty with the Sultan of Jahore, on the nearby mainland, which led to the establishment of the British trading settlement that has now grown into one of the world's most successful commercial centres. You only have to make a 360-degree turn to take in most of that history, old and new. Facing the white statue are the elegant classical colonial buildings that today house the parliament and government of the independent state. Beyond them is the inevitable cricket pitch, together with those other relics of the British past, the Anglican cathedral, the war memorial and, of course, the great hotel named after Raffles himself. This is a place of shady verandas and courtyards, and handsome public rooms cooled by overhead fans, where you have to sip a Singapore Sling at least once in your life.

Turn the other way, and see the view behind Raffles that he could never have imagined even in his wildest dreams of commercial success. There before you rises the new Singapore, on a breathtaking scale, with needle-tower skyscrapers glittering in the sunlight, an image of ice and fire that rivals – some would say surpasses – Manhattan. Yet, look closer and you will see, running along South Boat Quay, a line of pretty Chinese shop-houses, with their fanciful turned-up roofs. This is the old Singapore, carefully preserved and now a fashionable eating street, with a long line of restaurants offering that amazing diversity which has made Singapore a gourmet's paradise. I ate there on my first evening, choosing Gina's Nonya Restaurant, where I was able to see if it was true that the real test of a nonya cook is the vegetable dishes, the ingredients of which must remain fresh and crisp despite the time needed to cook a richly flavoured sauce. Chinese stir-fried vegetable dishes are instantly flavoured with liquid soy, while Indian cooks prefer durable ingredients, pulses and root vegetables that can be stewed until the hard dry spices have surrendered their tastes. Nonya food tries to have the best of both worlds. For Nonya Chap Chai (page 183), soft vegetables like mangetout and black fungus mushroom are quickly stir-fried with red beancurd, which is fermented and therefore already highly flavoured (see page 19). This is why nonya cooks use shrimp paste, introduced into Malay cuisine from the north, mixed with chilli and shallots to create Sambal Kaehand Panjang (see page 176), a prawn and long-bean sambal in which the prawn does not go mushy and the beans remain al dente.

However, I mustn't give the impression that eating in Singapore is only about dining in fashionable restaurants. For all its modernity, it is still very much an Asian city, and that means markets and food stalls and hawkers. Indeed, you have only to walk a short way from Raffles's Statue towards Cavanagh Bridge to find a cluster of stalls under a shady canopy. There I immediately went after what some call Kai Chok and others call Hainanese chicken (see page 173), a dish of boiled chicken with rice cooked in the stock, the apparent simplicity of which reveals much about the nature of Singaporean cuisine. As its second name implies, this recipe came from the island of Hunan off the southern coast of China. Most Chinese immigrants were from similar poor provinces, whose people most needed to find a new life elsewhere, and inevitably they brought with them a tradition of plain cooking, the product of restricted agriculture and limited ingredients. Once they were among the abundance of Southeast Asia, and such simple dishes were in the hands of their local wives, a transformation took place. Thus the Hainanese chicken that I ate on North Boat Quay came with a fiery dip of yellow bean sauce, ginger and chopped tiny 'bird's-eye' chillies, accompanied by a side dish of fresh cucumber and coriander, enough to turn a basic peasant meal into something quite special.

It isn't just Peranakan inventiveness that makes a Singapore food centre quite different from the rough-and-ready establishments found elsewhere in Southeast Asia. In Singapore someone has stopped to think about the situation. The protective arcade will have been built by the city authorities, who will also have provided decent sanitation, both lavatories and washrooms for the public, along with well-maintained cleaning facilities for the stall-holders, who will be subject to strict hygiene regulations.

This was most evident the following day, when I set off to eat at the famous Lau Pa Sat Festival Market, a Victorian-style food hall modelled on London's Covent Garden. At first I was disappointed to find it closed for renovation, but quickly saw that there was a large temporary arcade just across the road, already bustling with lunch-time refugees from banks and offices in the nearby tower blocks. There were so many stalls and such a variety of national cuisines on offer that customers were able to pick and mix between stalls as they fancied.

The same was true of the noodles, of which Singapore has some quite amazing varieties. One stall was selling basic quick-dipped white noodles with a dazzling array of deep-fried ingredients. The local laksa (see page 11) is a round rice noodle about the size of spaghetti, making it larger and more filling than most Asian pastas, yet here it was served with a choice of battered prawns, fish ball, hard-boiled eggs, beancurd, slices of red cuttlefish or vegetable tempura. Diners selected from among all these as they queued for the hot noodles, and a ladleful of rich stock.

After lunch, I took a bus out to the Haw Pa Villa Dragon World, a sort of Chinese Disneyland built by the brothers who made a fortune out of their famous Tiger Balm, the camphor-based ointment for aches and pains that is sold everywhere. Sadly, the journey through a dragon into the Chinese vision of Hell and the tableaux depicting scenes from Chinese mythology were less

Carefully restored Chinese Street off Orchard Road, Singapore

moving than those glimpses of real life that I'd seen in Hoi An or the Penang Museum. In truth I was more impressed by the bus ride to and from the villa. Imagine a clean, efficient, right-on-time, cheap system of public transport anywhere in the world today! Of course, there are many who say this kind of efficiency is the result of an intolerant and authoritarian system, but having visited many other Asian towns I find it hard to criticize. For me it was glorious to be riding along, upstairs on a British-style double-decker bus, and looking down on clean streets, well-manicured gardens, labourers carefully picking up rubbish. This is what I want for my own country and not a lot of silly talk about dirt being fun!

In fact, Singapore is heaven for those like me who prefer a mix of culture and cooking, because there the two always come side by side. When I headed off down Serangoon Road, the main street of the India Quarter, to see the Sri Veeramakalimiamman Temple, I found myself surrounded by restaurants and food shops. The temple itself is a fantastical world of gods, goddesses, demons and warriors, all fighting, dancing and love-making. Every surface is encrusted with brightly painted figures, a dream far more inventive than anything at the Haw Pa Villa or, indeed, in Disneyland.

It is all the more intriguing for also being inhabited by real people. Bare-chested Brahmin priests make ceaseless rounds of the shrines, bringing out the sacred fire so that worshippers can 'wash' themselves in its flames, draping the deities with garlands presented by supplicants, and taking offerings of fruit back into the sacred enclosure. This is all done in a slightly bored, matter-of-fact manner which implies that religion is just another part of life, as natural as eating and sleeping, the sort of thing you pop in and do whenever you have a moment. Hinduism has its roots in the earliest of mankind's religious practices and watching the little ceremonies carried out before a whole pantheon of gods and goddesses one sees the sort of things that must have taken place at the world's oldest shrines before recorded history.

Right outside the temple was a restaurant with a street-side cook, making nans and chapatis on a hot plate, just like that village bread maker in Burma. This was a fast-food place. I pointed to one of a dozen bubbling dishes, then went to wash my hands at a nearby tap while someone filled a small dish and brought me a fresh chapati and a jug of water. I had a mutton masala and a side plate of lentil dhal. With the temple opposite and the sari merchants and gold sellers on either side, I could have been in India, had it not been for the skyscrapers peeping over the roof-line, reminding me that this was Singapore after all.

From the moment you arrive, Singaporeans of whatever origin never stop telling you that you must eat chilli crab out on the East Coast – so I did. A friend and I arrived there by taxi and picked one of the sea-front restaurants at random, getting a table on the outside where we could watch the light fade over the Straits of Singapore and enjoy the refreshing breeze that always comes off the sea as night approaches. The flickering lights of dozens of tankers and container ships were both beautiful and a powerful reminder of Singapore's commercial might. As for the food – yes, it was worth it. We had chilli crab, which wasn't as killer-hot as we'd

imagined, with lots of sweet flavours too (see page 175), and deep-fried squid, which was equally terrific. All around us contented diners feasted on ginger fish and drunken prawns, a dish in which the creatures are left to swim in brandy, drinking as much as they can, before being grilled.

This left only the one culinary experience I'd been promising myself since I arrived, a full nonya meal. For that I chose the aptly named Nonya and Baba Restaurant (where else?) on River Valley Road. The restaurant is a long-time survivor in a city given to rapid changes of fashion because it is one of the rare places where you really can get Peranakan home cooking. The owner, Johnny Yeo, is himself the real thing, having a Chinese father and an Indonesian mother – who was herself a mix of Chinese and Indonesian. Her beautifully embroidered robes are displayed in the main dining room, along with photos of Elvis – Johnny is a great fan, as are countless Asians of his generation, my mother included. I am happy to say I ate like a hero: itek tim, a classic Peranakan duck dish with salted vegetable soup, perked up with mashed green chillies; Satay Ayam (page 179), made only with fresh – never frozen – chicken, that is first simmered in a special sauce of chilli, lemon grass, coconut and lime leaves, before being grilled. Then a touch of the family's Indonesian past, Ayam Buah Keluak, a pot roast of chicken and tamarind. Of course, I wasn't alone, otherwise all this would have been too much even for me, and with a circle of friends I was able to sample Otak Otak, a spicy fish paste barbecued in banana leaf, before finally ending up with Gula Melaka (sago pudding), and Kueh Pisang (banana pudding, see page 186).

The walk back to the hotel – well actually to the Chinese pub near the hotel – was a wise move and offered time to reflect on some of the things I've tried to recall in this book. To travel round Southeast Asia as I have done, from Laos to Singapore, is to move from yesterday to tomorrow, from the sealed-off world that is Burma to the newly opened-up Vietnam, with Cambodia hovering between the two. There is still plenty of time to see the past, and it is wonderful to experience the tranquil beauty of village life and to share a world that moves at the pace of the Temple seasons, but the people who live that life have a right to the things that we take for granted: education and less back-breaking labour and above all a clean healthy environment – and that means change. When it does come, I hope it will produce something not unlike Singapore.

As we walked back up the quiet garden slope towards the bustle of Orchard Road, we passed along some quite dark streets with dense bushes on either side, and at one point a woman on her own walked past with a smile and a cheerful 'Goodnight'. It took a moment before I realized with a jolt that she had not shown the slightest concern, and had been completely at ease, sure that she was safe, even on that lonely half-lit path. In how many cities across the world would that have been the case? Oh, yes, give me Singapore any day or night.

**Fishing boats on the
western coast near Penang**

LAKSA LEMAK
SPICY NOODLE SOUP

INGREDIENTS

- 3 large dried red chillies, finely chopped
- 1 stalk of lemon grass, finely chopped
- 1 teaspoon finely chopped galangal
- ½ teaspoon finely chopped fresh turmeric
- 8 small red shallots, finely chopped
- 1 teaspoon shrimp paste (see page 14)
- 1 tablespoon oil
- 225ml (8fl oz) coconut milk
- 1 litre (1¾ pints) vegetable stock (see page 14)
- 1 teaspoon tamarind water (see page 19)
- 1 tablespoon sugar
- 115g (4oz) raw prawns, peeled and deveined
- 115g (4oz) fish ball (see page 19)
- 2 tablespoons fish sauce
- 115g (4oz) beansprouts
- 225g (8oz) medium flat rice flour noodles (see page 11)

FOR THE GARNISH:

- 60g (2oz) fresh pineapple, cut into small segments then finely chopped
- 4 small red shallots, thinly sliced
- 10 mint leaves
- 4 small fresh red or green chillies, finely chopped

This will make two large bowls of soup noodles, enough for two if taken as a one-dish meal or four if part of a larger meal.

PREPARATION

In a mortar, pound together the chillies, lemon grass, galangal, turmeric and shallots to form a paste. Stir in the shrimp paste.

In a large heavy-based pan, heat the oil and stir in the paste. Add the coconut milk, stir well, then add the stock and bring to the boil. Add the tamarind water, sugar, prawns, fish ball and fish sauce. Turn down the heat and simmer.

In the meantime, heat a second pan of water and, when boiling, use a long-handled mesh strainer to dip the beansprouts in the water for a few seconds. Lift out, drain and place in 2 or 4 serving bowls (see above). Repeat this procedure with the noodles, blanching for a few seconds only. Drain, then place in the bowls.

Pour the soup into the bowls. Garnish with pineapple, shallots, mint and chilli, and serve.

KAI CHOK
HAINANESE CHICKEN

INGREDIENTS
- 1 medium chicken, about 1.5kg (3¼lb), preferably free-range or corn-fed
- 6 garlic cloves, lightly crushed
- ½ teaspoon salt
- 450g (1lb) rice, washed
- ½ cucumber, sliced, to serve
- 2 spring onions, finely chopped
- A large handful of coriander leaves to serve
- A sprinkling of ground black pepper

FOR THE HOT SAUCE:
- ½ tablespoon yellow bean sauce (see page 14)
- 2 teaspoons finely chopped ginger
- 3 garlic cloves, finely chopped
- 5 small fresh red or green chillies, finely chopped
- 1 teaspoon dark soy sauce
- 2 tablespoons light soy sauce
- 2 tablespoons rice vinegar
- 1 tablespoon sugar

PREPARATION
Place the chicken in a large pan and just cover with cold water. Remove the chicken and set aside.

Place 4 of the garlic cloves in the water with the salt and bring to the boil. When the water is boiling, return the chicken to the pan and boil for 20 minutes. Then lower the heat and simmer for 10 minutes. Remove the chicken and place on a rack to drain completely.

Place the rice in a medium pan and add enough of the chicken stock so that the liquid is 2.5cm (1in) above the level of the rice. Add the remaining 2 garlic cloves, cover the pan and bring to the boil. Uncover and stir. Then cover and turn down the heat to a minimum and gently simmer for 20 minutes without lifting the lid, after which the rice should have absorbed all the liquid and be fluffy, with each grain separate. Remove from the heat, cover and set aside. Make the hot sauce: in a small bowl, mix together all the ingredients, then set aside. Prepare a small plate of sliced cucumber and chopped coriander leaves and set aside. Carefully carve the chicken into thin slices, retaining any skin but discarding the bones. Set aside.

Reheat the remaining stock and pour into individual soup bowls for each diner, sprinkle with the spring onions and a little black pepper and put on the table along with the bowl of hot sauce and the plate of cucumber and coriander. Take a plate for each diner, place a good serving of rice on each, cover the rice with slices of chicken and serve. Everyone eats their own rice and chicken and sips their own soup – or pours a little over the rice if they wish – while they share the sauce and cucumber.

DAGING LEMBU GORENG CINA
BEEF STIR-FRIED WITH GINGER AND SPRING ONIONS

INGREDIENTS
- 2 garlic cloves, finely chopped
- 450g (1lb) fillet of beef, thinly sliced
- 1 teaspoon cornflour
- 1 egg
- 1 tablespoon oyster sauce
- 2 tablespoons oil
- 1 teaspoon finely chopped ginger
- 5 spring onions, coarsely chopped
- 1 tablespoon fish sauce
- A sprinkling of ground black pepper

PREPARATION
Place the garlic, beef, cornflour, egg and oyster sauce in a bowl, stir well and leave to marinate for 30 minutes.

Heat the oil in a wok or deep frying pan and fry the ginger briefly. Add the marinated beef and stir-fry until just cooked through.

Add all the remaining ingredients with 3 tablespoons water, stirring constantly.

As soon as the pepper is stirred in, remove from the heat and serve.

CILI KETMA

CHILLI CRAB

INGREDIENTS

- 4 fresh medium crabs
- 1 tablespoon finely chopped ginger
- 3 garlic cloves, finely chopped
- 4 fresh red or green chillies, finely chopped
- 1 teaspoon shrimp paste (see page 14)
- 4 tablespoons oil
- 2 tablespoons tomato purée
- 1 tablespoon fish sauce
- 1 tablespoon light soy sauce
- 1 teaspoon sugar

This is the one dish all Singaporeans insist you must eat, preferably at a seaside restaurant. It isn't as fearsomely hot as its name suggests – chilli is balanced by the sweetness of the tomato purée and sugar.

PREPARATION

If you buy live crabs, put the point of a knife into the shell between the eyes and strike the end of the handle a quick, hard blow – this kills the crab instantly and humanely. Cut away the undershell and discard the abdominal sac just behind the mouth. Break off the two large pincers and crack them open. With a Chinese chopper, quarter each crab. Set aside.

In a mortar, pound together the ginger, garlic and chillies to make a paste. Stir in the shrimp paste. Heat the oil in a wok or deep frying pan and fry the paste. Stir in the tomato purée and 2 tablespoons water. Add the crab pieces and stir well. Add the fish sauce, soy sauce and sugar and stir well, ensuring that the pieces are well coated. Turn out on a platter and serve.

KERANG TUMIS DENGAN CILI

MUSSELS WITH ONION, GARLIC AND CHILLI

INGREDIENTS

- 2 tablespoons oil
- 2 garlic cloves, finely chopped
- 4 small red shallots, thinly sliced
- 1 tablespoon finely chopped ginger
- 3 madium fresh red chillies, finely chopped
- 1 tablespoon yellow bean sauce (see page 14)
- 450g (1lb) mussels

Mussels should always be cleaned in several changes of water, with any that float being discarded. The principle is that those that are open before cooking must be thrown away, as should any that aren't open after cooking. Leave them overnight in a bucket of water with a good shake of porridge oats for them to feed on, they will eat and void themselves. Before cooking, you pull away the tiny beard and give the shells a good scrub to remove any barnacles.

PREPARATION

Heat the oil in a heavy-based pan which has a tight-fitting lid. Fry the garlic until golden. Add the shallots, ginger, chillies and bean sauce, and stir briefly.

Lift the mussels out of their last cleaning water and put them in the pan – any water that transfers with them should be enough for cooking purposes, but add a little more if you think the pan is too dry. Give the mussels one good stir. Cover the pan, turn up the heat and let them cook briefly – no more than 3 minutes, shaking the pan from time to time to ensure they cook evenly. Lift the lid to check all are open and discard any that are not.

Ensure each mussel gets a little of the sauce, then turn into bowls and serve.

SAMBAL KAEHAND PANJANG
PRAWN AND LONGBEAN SAMBAL

INGREDIENTS

- 2 large dried red chillies, finely chopped
- 8 small red shallots, finely chopped
- ½ teaspoon shrimp paste (see page 14)
- 2 tablespoons oil
- 2 tablespoons crushed peanuts
- 225g (8oz) raw prawns, peeled and deveined
- 225g (8oz) longbeans
- 125ml (4fl oz) coconut milk
- ½ teaspoon salt
- 1 teaspoon sugar

PREPARATION

In a mortar, pound together the chillies and shallots. Add the shrimp paste and mix well.

Heat the oil in a wok or deep frying pan and fry the paste. Add the peanuts and prawns. Stir well, then add the longbeans cut into 2.5cm (1in) lengths, coconut milk, salt and sugar.

Stir well for a few seconds, then turn into a bowl and serve.

SAMBAL IKAN
FISH SAMBAL

INGREDIENTS

- 2 small whole fish with rich 'meaty' flesh (such as mackerel)
- Oil for deep-frying
- 4 garlic cloves, finely chopped
- 8 small red shallots, coarsely chopped
- 1 stalk of lemon grass, finely chopped
- 3 large dried red chillies, finely chopped
- ½ teaspoon shrimp paste (see page 14)
- 2 teaspoons tamarind water (see page 19)
- 1 tablespoon sugar
- 1 tablespoon fish sauce

PREPARATION

Clean the fish and place in a deep pan. Add enough oil to come halfway up the fish, heat and fry the fish until it is golden brown, turning once. Remove, drain and place on a serving dish. Keep warm.

In a mortar, pound together the garlic, shallots, lemon grass and chillies to form a paste. Stir in the shrimp paste.

Put 2 tablespoons of the oil from the deep-frying into another frying pan, heat and stir in the paste. Add the tamarind water, 2 teaspoons water, the sugar and fish sauce.

Stir well, pour over the fried fish and serve.

FOO YONG HAI
CRAB MEAT AND BAMBOO SHOOT OMELETTE

INGREDIENTS

- 4 eggs
- 115g (4oz) cooked crab meat
- 115g (4oz) bamboo shoots, finely chopped
- 2 spring onions, finely chopped
- 1 tablespoon fish sauce
- ½ teaspoon sugar
- ¼ teaspoon black pepper
- 2 tablespoons oil

PREPARATION

In a bowl, beat the eggs and stir in all the ingredients except the oil.

Heat the oil in a frying pan and, when it is very hot, pour in the mixture. Leave to cook until the base of the omelette is firm and golden brown. Turn the omelette over and cook the other side in the same way.

Slide the omelette out on to a plate and serve.

SATAY AYAM
CHICKEN SATAY

INGREDIENTS

- 450g (1lb) chicken breast, preferably from a free-range or corn-fed bird
- 2 teaspoons coriander seeds
- ½ teaspoon cumin seeds
- 2 garlic cloves, coarsely chopped
- 1 teaspoon finely chopped ginger
- 1 teaspoon finely chopped fresh turmeric
- 4 small red shallots, finely chopped
- 1 teaspoon salt
- 2 tablespoons sugar
- 2 tablespoons oil
- 20 bamboo satay sticks, or equivalent

FOR THE SAUCE:

- 2 large dried red chillies, finely chopped
- 2 garlic cloves, finely chopped
- 1 stalk of lemon grass, finely chopped
- 1 teaspoon finely chopped fresh turmeric
- 2 tablespoons oil
- 450ml (¾ pint) coconut milk
- 1 tablespoon tamarind water (see page 19)
- 2 tablespoons sugar
- ½ teaspoon salt
- 4 tablespoons crushed peanuts

PREPARATION

If necessary, skin the chicken breasts and cut the meat away from the bone, then slice the meat into long thin strips, about 10×1cm (4×½in). Set aside.

In a mortar, pound together the coriander and cumin seeds, garlic, ginger, turmeric and shallots to make a paste. Stir in the salt, sugar and oil. Turn the mixture into a bowl, add the chicken strips and stir to coat thoroughly. Leave to marinate for 1 hour.

While the chicken is marinating, make the sauce: in a mortar, pound together the chilli, garlic, lemon grass and turmeric to form a paste.

Heat the oil in a wok or deep frying pan and stir in the paste. Add the coconut milk, stir well and bring to the boil. Add all the remaining ingredients in succession, stirring between each addition. Simmer for 3 minutes, then turn into a bowl.

When the chicken is marinated, fold each strip of chicken in a ripple and pierce this with a satay stick, through the folds as if sewing. Place the sticks under a hot grill or on a barbecue and turn from time to time, until cooked through. Serve with the sauce.

EGG SAMBAL
EGGS IN SPICY TOMATO SAUCE

INGREDIENTS

- 2 large dried red chillies, coarsely chopped
- 1 teaspoon finely chopped ginger
- 3 garlic cloves, finely chopped
- 8 small red shallots, finely chopped
- 3 tablespoons oil
- 5 tablespoons tomato purée
- 6 hard-boiled eggs, shelled
- 8 tablespoons coconut milk
- 2 teaspoons lemon juice
- 2 tablespoons sugar
- 1 teaspoon salt

A sambal is a very spicy side dish meant to add zest to other food. There should be at least one sambal with a well-balanced Malaysian meal.

PREPARATION

In a mortar, pound together the chillies, ginger, garlic and shallots to form a paste. Heat the oil in a wok or deep frying pan and stir in the paste. Add the tomato purée and stir well. Add the whole hard-boiled eggs and stir, coating well. Pour in the coconut milk and stir well. Add all the remaining ingredients, stir and simmer for 5 minutes. Turn into a bowl and serve.

SUP TAUHU
BEANCURD SOUP

INGREDIENTS
* 450ml (¾ pint) vegetable stock (see page 14)
* 115g (4oz) white beancurd, diced into 1cm (½in)cubes
* 30g (1oz) carrots, finely diced
* 30g (1oz) onion, finely diced
* 1 spring onion, thinly sliced
* 2 tablespoons light soy sauce
* 1 teaspoon sugar
* A sprinkling of freshly ground black pepper

This is my version of the soup served on the Eastern and Oriental Express. It is very mild and could be served, in the Asian way, not as a separate course but as part of a main course, a useful foil to a hot curry.

PREPARATION
Heat the stock, add the beancurd and bring to the boil. Stir in all the other ingredients except the pepper and serve.

MEE HOON GORENG
SINGAPORE FRIED NOODLES

INGREDIENTS
* 2 tablespoons oil
* 1 garlic clove, finely chopped
* 1 teaspoon curry powder (see page 15)
* 60g (2oz) small fresh shrimps
* 60g (2oz) barbecued pork (see page 183), cut into small cubes
* 1 egg, lightly beaten
* 225g (8oz) rice vermicelli (see page 11)
* 60g (2oz) beansprouts
* 60g (2oz) carrots, cut into thin matchsticks
* 1 tablespoon fish sauce
* 1 tablespoon light soy sauce
* 1 teaspoon sugar
* A sprinkling of black pepper

PREPARATION
Heat the oil in a wok or deep frying pan and fry the garlic until it is golden. Add the remaining ingredients in succession, stirring well between each addition.

As soon as the pepper is stirred in, turn out on a plate and serve.

RENDANG

BEEF RENDANG CURRY

INGREDIENTS
- 2 large dried red chillies, coarsely chopped
- 4 garlic cloves, coarsely chopped
- 1 tablespoon finely chopped ginger
- 1 tablespoon finely chopped galangal
- 1 stalk of lemon grass, finely chopped
- 1 teaspoon pounded coriander seeds
- ½ teaspoon ground cumin
- 2 tablespoons oil
- 450g (1lb) rump steak, cubed
- 450ml (¾ pint) coconut milk
- 1 medium onion, coarsely chopped
- 1 tablespoon tamarind water (see page 19)
- 1 tablespoon sugar
- 1 teaspoon salt

Rendang is a Sumatran dish that has spread throughout Malaysia and now has several variations – this is a standard 'wet' version with coconut milk; others are dryer and hotter.

PREPARATION

In a mortar, pound together the chilli, garlic, ginger, galangal and lemon grass to make a paste. Add the pounded coriander seeds and ground cumin. Mix well.

Heat the oil in a wok or deep frying pan and stir in the paste. Add the beef and stir well until just cooked through.

Add the coconut milk and stir well. Add all the remaining ingredients, stir, simmer for 30 minutes, then serve.

ROTI

PUFFED BREAD

INGREDIENTS
- 350g (12oz) plain flour
- 2 tablespoons sugar
- 1 egg, lightly beaten
- 6 tablespoons oil (you may not need all of this)

Roti is usually eaten as a savoury accompaniment to any sort of curry-style dish – the Beef Rendang (see above) would be perfect. In Asia roti is often served instead of rice for a light meal. Traditionally it was also a form of cutlery – you used the roti to scoop up the meat dish. You can also eat it as a sweet, however, like a sort of thick crêpe. As children we ate it with sugar or condensed milk. Roti is best cooked on any kind of flat griddle, but a flat frying pan will do.

PREPARATION

Put the flour in a bowl, sprinkle in the sugar and mix well. Pour the egg into the flour and mix well, then gradually add 225ml (8fl oz) water, kneading with your fingers to make a smooth dough. Divide the dough into 10 balls.

On a floured board, press out each ball to make a round pancake – this should be as thin as possible, yet still hold together when lifted from the board.

Heat a griddle or frying pan, put in just enough oil to grease the surface and, when this is sizzling hot, fry the pancakes, turning once. The roti will slightly bubble as it cooks, creating a mottled effect; overall both sides should be a crisp golden brown with darker brown patches. Continue until all are cooked.

NONYA CHAP CHAI

NONYA MIXED VEGETABLES

INGREDIENTS

- 2 tablespoons oil
- 2 garlic cloves, finely chopped
- 1 teaspoon red beancurd (see page 19)
- 1 medium onion, thinly sliced
- 60g (2oz) Chinese cabbage, coarsely chopped
- 60g (2oz) carrots, coarsely chopped
- 60g (2oz) black fungus mushroom, soaked, drained and coarsely chopped (see page 19)
- 60g (2oz) mangetout, topped and tailed and the hard spine cut away
- 2 tablespoons water
- 115g (4oz) cellophane noodles, soaked and drained (see page 11)
- 60g (2oz) beancurd sheets, broken into small pieces and soaked in water for 2–3 minutes (see page 19)
- 2 tablespoons light soy sauce
- 1 teaspoon sugar
- ½ teaspoon ground black pepper

PREPARATION

Heat the oil in a wok or deep frying pan, then add and stir-fry all the ingredients in succession, stirring once between each addition.

  After stirring in the pepper, turn out on a dish and serve.

CHAR SIEW

BARBECUED PORK

INGREDIENTS

- 4 tablespoons tomato purée
- 2 tablespoons dark soy sauce
- 4 tablespoons light soy sauce
- 4 tablespoons sugar
- 1kg (2¼lb) pork belly strips
- Cucumber slices, short lengths of spring onion and quarters of hard-boiled egg to garnish
- A little chopped chilli in rice vinegar or wine vinegar to serve (optional)

FOR THE SAUCE:

- 450ml (¾ pint) pork stock (see page 14)
- 2 tablespoons light soy sauce
- 3 tablespoons sugar
- 2 tablespoons fish sauce
- 1 teaspoon rice flour

PREPARATION

In a large bowl, mix the tomato purée, soy sauces and sugar. Add the pork belly strips and stir well to coat evenly. Leave to marinate for 1 hour.

  Place the marinated pork belly strips on a barbecue or under a preheated grill and turn them from time to time until well cooked through. While the pork is cooking, make the sauce: heat the stock in a saucepan, add all the ingredients except the rice flour and stir well. Bring to the boil and simmer for 1 minute. Sprinkle the rice flour over the liquid and stir gently until it thickens.

  Slice the pork very thinly before serving. (In the West, it is often cut rather thickly, whereas in Asia it is always sliced as thinly as sliced ham.)

  Put a heap of rice on a plate and top with thin slices of barbecued pork. Pour over a good helping of the sauce and garnish with sliced cucumber, one or two short lengths of spring onion and a quartered hard-boiled egg. A little chopped chilli in rice vinegar or wine vinegar can also be served as an accompaniment.

GADO GADO

VEGETABLE SALAD WITH PEANUT SAUCE

INGREDIENTS

- Oil for deep-frying
- 2 blocks of beancurd, about 5cm (2in) square
- 115g (4oz) beansprouts
- 115g (4oz) longbeans, chopped into 2.5cm (1in) lengths
- 115g (4oz) cucumber, thinly sliced
- 115g (4oz) white cabbage, thinly sliced then broken up into strands
- 2 hard-boiled eggs

FOR THE PEANUT SAUCE:

- 2 large dried red chillies, finely chopped
- 2 garlic cloves, finely chopped
- 5 small red shallots, finely chopped
- ½ teaspoon shrimp paste (see page 14)
- 2 tablespoons oil
- 450ml (¾ pint) coconut milk
- ½ teaspoon salt
- 1 tablespoon sugar
- 1 teaspoon tamarind water (see page 19)
- 4 tablespoons crushed peanuts

PREPARATION

First make the sauce: in a mortar, pound together the chillies, garlic and shallots to form a paste. Add the shrimp paste and mix well.

Heat the oil in a wok or deep frying pan and stir in the paste. Add the coconut milk and stir well. Add all the remaining ingredients together, stirring well. Cook briefly until the coconut milk comes to the boil. Remove at once from the heat.

Make the salad: heat the oil and deep-fry the beancurd until golden. Remove, drain and set aside.

Arrange all the vegetables in a salad bowl. Shell the eggs and quarter them, then place in the salad bowl. Thinly slice the beancurd and place the slices in the bowl.

Serve with the sauce, either separately or poured over the salad and tossed.

OPOR AYAM

CHICKEN IN COCONUT

INGREDIENTS

- 1 medium chicken, about 1.25kg (2¾lb)
- 1 teaspoon coriander seeds
- ½ teaspoon cumin seeds
- 2 large dried red chillies, coarsely chopped
- 1 tablespoon finely chopped galangal
- 3 garlic cloves, finely chopped
- 1 teaspoon finely chopped ginger
- 1 teaspoon finely chopped fresh turmeric
- 8 small red shallots, finely chopped
- 3 tablespoons oil
- 1 stalk of lemon grass, chopped into 2.5cm (1in) lengths and slightly crushed
- 700ml (1¼ pints) coconut milk
- 4 kaffir lime leaves, coarsely chopped
- 2 teaspoons salt
- 1 tablespoon sugar

PREPARATION

Prepare the chicken: chop off the wings and legs, cut the carcass in half lengthways, then quarter it across; chop each quarter into 4 (you should now have 20 pieces of chicken). Set aside.

In a mortar, pound the coriander seeds, then add the cumin seeds and pound together. Add the chillies, galangal, garlic, ginger, turmeric and shallots and pound to form a paste.

Heat the oil in a large heavy-based pan and stir in the paste. Add the lemon grass and stir. Add 4 tablespoons of the coconut milk and stir. Add the chicken pieces and stir well. Add a further 6 tablespoons of the coconut milk and continue stirring. Add the kaffir lime leaves, salt and sugar, and stir. Add the remaining coconut milk and simmer for 30 minutes.

Turn into a bowl and serve.

PULOT HITAM
BLACK STICKY RICE PUDDING

INGREDIENTS
- 225g (8oz) black sticky rice (see page 11)
- 115g (4oz) white sticky rice
- 85g (3oz) sugar

TO SERVE:
- 225ml (8fl oz) coconut cream
- A pinch of salt

This is called black sticky rice pudding because the colour that predominates comes from the dark husk on the unpolished grains. Because these are too hard to use on their own, however, they have to be mixed with the much softer white grains. Nevertheless, it makes that very rare thing, a healthy pudding, as the husk is the most nutritious part of the grain.

Although I ate this in a restaurant in Singapore, it is eaten in homes all over Southeast Asia, and much loved by children because of its mix of sugary rice with slightly salty cream.

PREPARATION
Soak both types of sticky rice overnight, or for at least 6 hours.

Wash and drain them, then place them in a pan with 1.5 litres (2¾ pints) water and bring to the boil. Simmer, stirring from time to time, until the grains have absorbed all the water but are not yet dry. Add the sugar and stir well.

Turn into bowls and pour over a little coconut cream mixed with salt.

KUEH PISANG
BANANA PUDDING

INGREDIENTS
- 1 large banana
- 400ml (14fl oz) coconut cream
- 1 teaspoon rice flour
- 3 tablespoons sugar
- A pinch of salt

This is another pudding from the Nonya and Baba Restaurant in Singapore, where they put a little of the banana and cream into banana leaf envelopes and then chill the packages before serving. I've given an easier method here.

PREPARATION
Cut the banana into thin rounds and divide between 4 ramekins or small soufflé dishes.

In a pan, heat the coconut cream and stir in the rice flour, sugar and salt. Simmer until the mixture thickens.

Pour the mixture over the banana, then put into the refrigerator to cool and thicken before serving.

MAKING A MEAL

The recipes in this book can be divided into four categories:

A One-dish meals. These are usually noodle or rice dishes that are for quick eating -- lunch, snacks etc.

B Starters (hors d'oeuvre, appetizers, party-food). Traditional meals did not have separate courses, but it was usual for certain spicy dishes to be prepared first and brought out to be enjoyed with drinks before the rest of the meal was ready. Today, these are often used as hors d'oeuvre in the Western manner.

C Main courses. While there are some national variations, a well-planned meal anywhere in Southeast Asia consists of a group of dishes that create a harmonious balance of tastes and textures -- liquid and dry, hot and sweet, cooked and raw, soft and crisp, fried and steamed. There should also be a variety of ingredients: meat, fish, seafood and vegetables.

D Desserts. Most often a Southeast Asian meal ends with whatever fruits are in season. As in the West, however, the creation of many desserts is a specialist craft and they are more often bought than made at home. However, I have included a few easy recipes which can be used to enliven a dinner party.

VEGETARIAN MEALS

The symbol (♥) indicates that a dish is (or, with only slight alteration, could easily be made to be) suitable for vegetarians. I have included eggs and some recipes call for fish sauce, which can be replaced by light soy sauce. Almost all stir-fried meals can be converted by the simple procedure of dropping the meat listed in the ingredients and replacing it with an equal weight of coarsely chopped chunky-fleshed mushrooms. Many Southeast Asian vegetarians cook a meal for themselves, separating a little of the vegetarian version on a plate, then adding meat last for a second version for any non-vegetarian guests.

DRINKS

In most parts of Southeast Asia, cool water was traditionally drunk after a family meal. Except for Muslim Malaysia, men enjoying a night out would take bottles of spirits -- whisky or brandy -- to a restaurant to be drunk before, during and after the meal, much diluted with ice. For Vietnamese and Singapore nonya meals, Chinese tea would be an appropriate drink. Today, however, those that can afford them tend to drink Western drinks with their meals -- beer, Coca-Cola and, increasingly, wine.

While common-sense dictates that it would be foolish to serve a subtle vintage with a fiery curry, most robust characterful wines, especially those from Australasia, go well with most dishes in this book. With snacks and lunches from stalls and street-hawkers, it is common to see people drinking iced tea and iced coffee, though visitors are well advised to be wary of ice where there is any doubt as to the purity of the water from which it was made.

RECIPE LISTS AND MENU PLANS

The following is a guide to how the recipes can be broken down then re-combined into a full meal for at least four people. If you have more guests, do not make extra amounts of these dishes but add some different ones from the lists. They are separated according to country to enable you to make an authentic Laotian or Burmese, etc., meal. There is much pleasure to be had, however, from picking out dishes from different countries and bringing them together as I have in the Southeast Asian feast that ends this section.

VIETNAM

Nem Cuon Song (Fresh 'Nem' Spring Roll) page 122

▼ **Cha Gio Chay** (Vegetarian Spring Roll) page 125

Sa Suon Chien (Deep-fried Spare Ribs with Chilli and Lemon Grass) page 129

Cang Cua Chien (Deep-fried Crab-claws with Pork and Prawn Envelope) page 125

BURMA

▼ **Bayagyaw** (Spicy Split-pea Fritters) page 153

▼ **Pyaung-Bu Gyaw** (Fried Sweetcorn with Crispy Shallots) page 145

MALAYSIA AND SINGAPORE

Satay Ayam (Chicken Satay) page 179

MAIN COURSES

To create a substantial meal for four, select at least one dish from each category and serve with rice.

THAILAND

Dips and Sauces

Nam Prik Gung Pow (Grilled Shrimp Spice Dip) page 48

Soups

Tom Yam Gai (Chicken and Lemon Grass Soup) page 32

Salads

Yam Krabi (Krabi Seafood Salad) page 38

Mian Pla (Fish Ginger and Lime Salad) page 38

Curries

Gaeng Kiow Wan Nua (Beef in Green Curry with Coconut) page 40

Gaeng Luang Pla (Yellow Curry Fish) page 43

Penang Gai (Penang Dry Curry Chicken) page 40

Fried Dishes

Pad Prik King Nua Pad Bung (Fried Beef with Morning Glory) page 43

Pad Pet Moo (Stir-fried Pork with Curry Paste) page 41

Steamed Dishes

Gam Poo Op (Steamed Crab Claws) page 32

Pla Nung Manao (Steamed Fish with Lime) page 44

LAOS

For a more authentic Laotian meal it would be preferable – but not essential – to serve sticky rice.

Soups

▼ **Keng Bouad Mak Fak Kham** (Pumpkin in Coconut Soup) page 64

Ped Tom Kah (Duck and Galangal Soup) page 64

Keng Kalampi (White Cabbage Soup) page 62

Salads

Yam Kai Tom (Boiled Chicken Salad) page 74

Laap Ngua (Spicy Beef Salad) page 67

▼ **Soop Houa Phak** (Cooked Vegetable Salad) page 68

Curries

Kalee Ped (Duck Curry) page 73

Fried Dishes

Kai Jeun Na Som (Sweet-and-sour Fried Eggs) page 73

Sousi Pla (Spicy Coconut Fish) page 75

Kai Pad Mak Phet Deng (Fried Chicken with Red Chilli) page 77

Ngua Pad Mak Khe Ua (Fried Beef with Aubergine) page 75

Pad Som Sin Moo (Lemon Pork) page 77

▼ **Hed Pad Som Phak** (Mushrooms Fried with Pickled Cabbage) page 77

Steamed Dishes

Mok Pla (Fish Curry Steamed in Banana Leaf) page 70

CAMBODIA

Dips and Sauces

▼ **Tik Marij** (Cambodian Pepper Dip) page 91

Tik Prahok (Pickled Fish Dip) page 94

Soups

▼ **Samlor Jruoh** (Hot-and-sour Mushroom and Tomato Soup) page 93

Salads

Plea Saj Go (Hot-and-sour Beef Salad) page 99

Yoam Makah Trey Ang (Deep-fried Smoked Fish with Raw Mango Salad) page 94

Curries

Samlor Tik Tumpeang (Fish, Coconut and Young Bamboo Shoot Soup) page 100

Fried Dishes

▼ **Trop Bamporng Jiamuay Pong Tia** (Fried Aubergine with Egg) page 96

Saj Go Tik Prahok (Beef and Raw Vegetables with Pickled Fish Dip) page 99

Op Jumnee Jruk Bamporng (Sweet-and-sour Spare Ribs) page 96

Loclac (Stir-fried Pork with Salad and Tik Marij) page 101

Trey Pramar Jamhoy (Omelette with Pork and Pickled Fish) page 100

Muan Dot (Pot-roasted Chicken with Lemon Grass) page 88

Muan Char Khyey (Chicken with Ginger) page 103

Muan Char Kreung (Chicken Fried with Curry Paste) page 103

Steamed Dishes

Aamoh (Steamed Fish Curry) page 101

VIETNAM

Salads

Nom Du Du Thit Bo Nuong (Grilled Beef with Raw Papaya Salad) page 126

Goi Ga (Chicken Salad with Mint and Nuts) page 122

Fried Dishes

Cha Ca Nam (Grilled Fish with Mushroom Sauce) page 130

Bo Xao Mang (Beef with Bamboo Shoots) page 117

Than Chan Chanh (Kidneys with Mint and Lime) page 120

▼ **Dau Phu Xao Rau** (Beancurd with Stir-fried Mixed Vegetables) page 128

Chim Cuoc Chien (Deep-fried Quail) page 126

Bo Cau Roti (Grilled Pigeon) page 128

Steamed Dishes

Tom Hap Mien Dong (Prawn and Vermicelli Hotpot) page 128

Ca Hap Nam (Steamed Fish with Mushrooms) page 126

BURMA

Dips and Sauces

Ngan-Bya-Ye Dhyaw (Burmese Hot Sauce) page 146

Soups

Thakhwa-Thi Hin-Gyo (Cucumber and Dried Shrimp Soup) page 150

Salads

▼ **Khayan-Gyin-Thi-Thoke** (Tomato Salad) page 149

▼ **Mon-La-Doke-Thoke** (White Cabbage Salad) page 146

Nga-Pe Thoke (Hot-and-sour Fishcake Salad) page 146

Curries and Spiced Vegetable Dishes

Pazun Hin (Prawn Curry) page 149

▼ **Hmyit-Kyaw** (Bamboo Shoots Stir-Fried with Spice Paste) page 149

▼ **Khayan-Thi Pyot-Kyaw** (Fried Aubergine with Chilli and Shallots) page 149

Fried Dishes

Wet Tauk-Tauk Gyaw (Pork Fried with Dried Chilli) page 145

Ngar-Asat-Kyaw (Fried Fish with Crispy Chilli, Garlic and Shallots) page 150

Seik-Tha Hin (Lamb with Mint Leaves) page 154

Ametha Hin (Beef in Tamarind Sauce) page 157

▼ **Pe-Gyan-Gyaw** (Twice-cooked Split-peas) page 154

Be-Gin (Crispy Duck) page 154

MALAYSIA AND SINGAPORE

Dips, Sauces and Sambals

Sambal Kaehang Panjang (Prawn and Longbean Sambal) page 176

Sambal Ikan (Fish Sambal) page 176

Egg Sambal (Eggs in Spicy Tomato Sauce) page 179

Soups

▼ **Sup Tauhu** (Beancurd Soup) page 180

Salads

▼ **Gado Gado** (Vegetable Salad with Peanut Sauce) page 185

Curries

Rendang (Beef Rendang Curry) page 182

Fried Dishes

▼ **Roti** (Puffed Bread) page 182

Opor Ayam (Chicken in Coconut) page 185

Char Siew (Barbecued Pork) page 183

▼ **Nonya Chap Chai** (Nonya Mixed Vegetables) page 183

Daging Lembu Goreng Cina (Beef Stir-fried with Ginger and Spring Onions) page 173
Cili Ketma (Chilli Crab) page 175
Foo Yong Hai (Crab Meat and Bamboo Shoot Omelette) page 176
Steamed Dishes
Kerang Tumis Dengan Cili (Mussels with Onion, Garlic and Chilli) page 175

DESSERTS

THAILAND

Kai Wan (Sweet Ginger Eggs) page 48
Kow Niew Tat (Sweet Sticky Rice Cakes) page 47

LAOS

Khao Tom Mak Kuay (Steamed Sticky Rice with Banana) page 78
Nam Van Loi Mak Teng (Melon in Coconut Milk) page 78

CAMBODIA

Bai Damnerb Gruop Khano (Grilled Sticky Rice with Coconut and Jackfruit) page 104

VIETNAM

Banh Chuoi (Banana and Sweet Potato Fritters) page 130
Che Dau Xanh (Moong Beans in Dark Sugar) page 129

BURMA

Mon-Let-Saung (Sago with Palm Sugar and Coconut Milk) page 158
Kyauk-kyaw (Jelly Custard) page 158

MALAYSIA AND SINGAPORE

Pulot Hitam (Black Sticky Rice Pudding) page 186
Kueh Pisang (Banana Pudding) page 186

SAMPLE MENUS

THAILAND

Starters
Jin Ping (Grilled Marinated Pork) page 35
Tod Man Gung (Deep-fried Prawn and Sweetcorn Cakes) page 44
Main Courses
Yam Krabi (Krabi Seafood Salad) page 38
Gaeng Kiow Wan Nua (Beef in Green Curry with Coconut) page 40
Pla Nung Manao (Steamed Fish with Lime) page 44
Dessert
Kow Niew Tat (Sweet Sticky Rice Cakes) page 47

LAOS

Starters
Sai Ua Moo (Pork Sausage) page 68
Laap Ngua (Spicy Beef Salad) page 67

Main Courses
Ped Tom Kah (Duck and Galangal Soup) page 64
Ngua Pad Mak Khe Ua (Fried Beef with Aubergine) page 75
Hed Pad Som Phak (Mushrooms Fried with Pickled Cabbage) page 77
Mok Paa (Fish Curry Steamed in Banana Leaf) page 70
Sticky Rice page 11
Dessert
Nam Van Loi Mak Teng (Melon in Coconut Milk) page 78

CAMBODIA

Starters
Samlor Chanang Dy (Clay-pot Beef, Vegetables and Noodle Soup) page 93
Yoam Makah Trey Ang (Deep-fried Smoked Fish with Raw Mango Salad) page 94
Main Courses
Samlor Tik Tumpeang (Fish, Coconut and Young Bamboo Shoot Soup) page 100
Trop Bamporng Jiamuay Pong Tia (Fried Aubergine with Egg) page 96
Jumnee Jruk Bamporng (Sweet-and-sour Spare Ribs) page 96
Muan Dot (Pot-roasted Chicken with Lemon Grass) page 88
Tik Marij (Cambodian Pepper Dip) page 91
Tik Prahok (Pickled Fish Dip) page 94
Dessert
Bai Damnerb Gruop Khano (Grilled Sticky Rice with Coconut and Jackfruit) page 104

VIETNAM

Starters
Nem Cuon Song (Fresh 'Nem' Spring Roll) page 122
Cang Cua Chien (Deep-fried Crab-Claws with Pork and Prawn Envelope) page 125
Main Courses
Cha Ca Nam (Grilled Fish with Mushroom Sauce) page 130
Than Chan Chanh (Kidneys with Mint and Lime) page 120
Chim Cuoc Chien (Deep-fried Quail) page 126
Tom Hap Mien Dong (Prawn and Vermicelli Hotpot) page 128
Dessert
Che Dau Xanh (Moong Beans in Dark Sugar) page 129

BURMA

Starters
Bayagyaw (Spicy Split-pea Fritters) page 153
Nga-Pe Thoke (Hot-and-sour Fishcake Salad) page 146
Main Courses
Pazun Hin (Prawn Curry) page 149
Wet Tauk-Tauk Gyaw (Pork Fried with Dried Chilli) page 145
Seik-Tha Hin (Lamb with Mint Leaves) page 154

Be-Gin (Crispy Duck) page 154
Ngan-Bya-Ye Dhyaw (Burmese Hot Sauce) page 146
Dessert
Kyauk-kyaw (Jelly Custard) page 158

MALAYSIA AND SINGAPORE

Starters
Satay Ayam (Chicken Satay) page 179
Gado Gado (Vegetable Salad with Peanut Sauce) page 185
Main Courses
Sup Tauhu (Beancurd Soup) page 180
Rendang (Beef Rendang Curry) page 182
Opor Ayam (Chicken in Coconut) page 185
Cili Ketma (Chilli Crab) page 175
Rice
Roti (Puffed Bread) page 182
Dessert
Pulot Hitam (Black Sticky Rice Pudding) page 186

SOUTHEAST ASIAN FEAST

Canapés
Thailand – **Gratong Mee Krob** (Crispy Noodle Baskets) page 36
Burma – **Bayagyaw** (Spicy Split-pea Fritters) page 153
Malaysia & Singapore – **Satay Ayam** (Chicken Satay) page 179
Hors d'oeuvres
Vietnam – **Nem Cuon Song** (Fresh 'Nem' Spring Roll) page 122
Dips and Sauces
Cambodia – **Tik Marij** (Cambodian Pepper Dip) page 91
Burma – **Ngan-Bya-Ye** Dhyaw (Burmese Hot Sauce) page 146
Soup
Thailand – **Tom Yam Gai** (Chicken and Lemon Grass Soup) page 32
Salad
Laos – **Laap Ngua** (Spicy Beef Salad) page 67
Curry
Burma– **Khayan-Thi Pyot-Kyaw** (Fried Aubergine with Chilli and Shallots) page 149
Fried Dishes
Vietnam – **Chim Cuoc Chien** (Deep-fried Quail) page 126
Burma – **Seik-Tha Hin** (Lamb with Mint Leaves) page 154
Malaysia & Singapore – **Nonya Chap Chai** (Nonya Mixed Vegetables) page 183
Steamed Dish
Vietnam – **Ca Hap Nam** (Steamed Fish with Mushrooms) page 126
Desserts
Laos – **Nam Van Loi Mak Teng** (Melon in Coconut Milk) page 78
Malaysia & Singapore – **Kueh Pisang** (Banana Pudding) page 186

Bon Appetit!

INDEX